D1708911

Amaretto

Amaretto

JOE UPTON

INTERNATIONAL MARINE PUBLISHING COMPANY
Camden, Maine

©1986 by International Marine Publishing Company

Typeset by The Key Word, Inc., Belchertown, Massachusetts
Printed and bound by Alpine Press, Stoughton, Massachusetts

Published by International Marine Publishing Company
21 Elm Street, Camden, Maine 04843
(207) 236-4342

Library of Congress Cataloging-in-Publication Data

Upton, Joe, 1946–
    Amaretto.

    1. Herring-fisheries—Maine.   2. Upton, Joe,
1946–   .   3. Amaretto (Ship).   I. Title.
SH351.H5U68 1986   639'.2755   86-10464
ISBN 0-87742-223-0

For
Mary Lou, Matthew, and Katherine Anne

Acknowledgments

Only because of the kindness and generosity of dozens of people along the Maine Coast did Amaretto work again. These are but a few of them.

To Junior Farrin, for offering me his wharf to lie at and work from, and for giving me encouragement when I needed it, which was often.

To Merrit Brackett, who spent a whole morning setting the valves and injectors of Amaretto's World War II surplus engine, and when I asked what I owed him, said, "Aw, I didn't do nothing; just give me five bucks."

To Stevie Kaimmer and Elin Elisofon, for many hours of dedicated and patient work both ashore and on the water.

To Henry Dodge of the carrier Pauline, and Clarence Grew of the carrier Delca, for their advice and encouragement on getting started in the business of carrying herring.

To Alfred Osgood and Bob Warren, herring fishermen, for their patience in working with us.

To the lobstermen of Vinalhaven, for giving a new player in an old boat a chance to break into a cutthroat business.

To my friend and fishing partner, Mike Mesko, for his help and advice, both on the boat and on the book.

To my editor, Jon Eaton, for tracking down this story and helping me make it into a book.

And last, but hardly least, to the builders of the Muriel, or Amaretto, mostly passed on now I suppose, for their craft in putting together such a vessel in 1918.

One

Seal Island: black, windy. We jogged bow up into the swell and the wind, watching three seiners, forty- and fifty-footers with piles of net ready on their sterns. They moved cautiously in toward the cliffs, dim shapes showing no lights that might spook the herring. Ann took the wheel while I pulled on a jacket and went out onto the stern to watch. The sky was black with dark red edges. To port and starboard the lights of the other sardine carriers rose and fell on the swells.

Now and again, carrying clearly out to us, we heard the boom of a big sea slamming into the cliffs.

The radio spoke: "I dunno, Joe, they're right in the rocks here. If I get a set out you'll have to get a line on me quick, and start towing or the wind'll carry us ashore. . . ."

Jim didn't sound too excited about setting his net, and I didn't blame him, for once a seiner has his net out, he is helpless, unable to move lest the twine tangle in the propeller. The cliffs seemed right in front of him, the wind and the tide pushing him on.

"Well, try it if you want. . . ." I sounded braver than I felt. Something about the place—the seas, the rising wind, the great cliffs—spooked me.

"OK, get ready then, I might let one go here pretty quick."

I turned the boat in toward the cliffs, and we rolled heavily for a minute until we got out of the trough.

Ann looked ahead at the dark cul de sac bordered by white water and black rock.

"We're going in *there*?"

I nodded, saying nothing.

The sky was dark, but the water had begun to fire brilliantly with phosphorescence, the wakes of the seiners glowing in the darkness. Now and then a big sea would pass beneath the boat, lifting us higher and higher, then dropping us into the trough, and it would slide on into the cliffs, hang there for a moment, brightly glowing water against the sheer black rock, then fall away to become darkness again.

A tiny light winked on—the end light on Jim's net; he was getting ready. Then his wake circled, and I could see a faint line of corks behind him as he set.

"Amaretto, get ready. As soon as I light up, c'mon in." Jim's voice was anxious.

We waited for him to purse his net and get the rings, the bottom, up, then he would turn on his deck lights and we would go in, throw him a line, and tow him away from the cliffs.

He lit up suddenly, and we could see dramatically the cliffs, very close behind him, towering over the boats. We headed in, Ann on the stern with a coil of line in her hand. The way the tide was running, we had to get the line to Jim on the first throw. His net would probably be caught on the rocks before we could get lined up for another try.

The toss was perfect, our line quickly made fast to their towing bridle. I gave Amaretto half throttle and started towing them away from the cliffs.

Only after what seemed like a very long time did the cliffs recede far enough for us to go in alongside him and dip a few hundred bushels of small bright herring out of his net.

Jim came aboard for a moment, looked into our hold, sighed, clearly without much enthusiasm for another set. "We can try it again . . . if you want. . . ."

I looked around. The wind seemed to be making up. The boats worked heavily together, crushing the big fenders, straining the lines.

I shrugged. The place made me uneasy, too. "Naw, I haven't got much courage either. This'll do us for tomorrow anyway," I lied.

The Nighthawk disappeared into the black and we were alone, cleaning up, hosing the herring scales off the deck, the sides of the house, and I was about to head up the bay for home when I noticed another seiner still there, circling right under the cliffs, and a carrier's lights off to the south.

I had thought that all the others had given it up as too risky, too rough. But whoever was left just patiently circled, even closer to the cliffs than Jim had been, waiting for his chance.

His net light winked on—the stranger was about to set. I waited, wanting to watch the outcome.

Twenty minutes passed, then his decklights came on, showing a white seiner, a circle of corks, and the cliffs close behind.

A totally relaxed voice came over the radio. "Henrrrrryyyy........"

"Gotcha." Another voice came back, and from the big sardine carrier offshore a brilliant spotlight stabbed the night, picking out the boat, the net, the sheer rock wall behind.

It looked as if they were almost ashore, his corks rubbing against the very rock wall, and then I realized what he must have been waiting for—that there must be a place there on the sheer cliff with deep water below. A place where you could set your net right against the cliffs with a sea running and not foul or hang up, the rock was so smooth, but just in that one place. And all that while, the skipper of the seiner had been watching the fish, waiting for them to slide into just that spot.

The carrier came in. I recognized her as the Pauline. I could see the line thrown, and the tow out from the cliffs begin.

Tired, I swung around the point and headed up the bay.

"Amaretto." The radio, that same lazy voice that had called the carrier in. It was David, and the Starlight; I now recognized his voice. "Don't run away. I got more here 'n Henry wants, so stick around and I'll load you. . . ." His voice trailed off.

"Sounds good. I'll swing back around. . . ."

So we turned and steamed the twenty minutes or so around to the back side of the island.

And when we came around the point, the other carrier, still pumping fish out

3

of the net, seen from a quarter of a mile away, seemed as if she was sinking. She was so low in the water, her lights made it look as if the only things sticking up were the bow and the pilothouse.

And there were *still* fish in the net. It was the biggest set I had ever seen. David had loaded a carrier twice our size when all the other boats had given it up for the night, and still had plenty left over to give us.

Gingerly, with all our fenders rigged, we slid alongside David's boat, took the corks, and began unloading herring out of his seine with our big dipnet. The cliffs were close, and the wind was pressing us on; it was not a time for words.

A paper cup of whiskey appeared in my hand, and then David was beside me, watching us work. He stooped to pick up a herring from the deck, looked at it for a moment, and turned to me, a short bull of a man in orange oilskins, with pale blue bloodshot eyes set in a young, tired-looking face.

He rubbed his fingers together, and they were covered with the shiny patina of herring scales.

"Fives," he said, "and lucky to get 'em."

He seemed totally relaxed, looking into our hold, watching it slowly fill, oblivious to the mean night and the rocky cliffs close at hand, the apprehensive people around him.

The whiskey felt good, easing the pain in my back from driving the heavy handle of the dipnet into the fish. We were hustling to get our load before the rocks got too close. David's crew said nothing, silent oilskin-clad figures working the net up, herding the fish toward the dipnet. But now and again, one of them would look over his shoulder at the island, rising and falling, a granite wall just visible at the edge of the circle of light, maybe twenty yards away and getting closer.

Then we were done, the hold almost full, exactly what we wanted. Ann quickly washed down the deck, lashed the boom back amidships, shoveled the last salt on top of the fish.

David put out a hand and one of his crew slapped the bottle into it. He refilled our cups. Ann was already untying the lines, anxious, as was I and everyone else except, apparently, David, about the cliff just off our sterns.

"Well," he said, stepping nimbly back aboard his boat just as it came even with us in the swell, "don't be a stranger. Call us anytime." He saluted us with his cup, waved to his men, and then the lines were off, their lights were out, and they slid away from the base of the cliff and disappeared into the night.

4

Two

It was on a hard day in the hardest kind of winter that the whole business with Seal Island and David began. The world was snow and wind, with sea smoke off the water, ice along the shore, and the first of the year yet to come.

From Alaska and five years in intensely competitive, high-technology fisheries, I had come to Maine and bought a sixty-year-old boat almost sight unseen to seek a quieter living on the sea.

There was but a borrowed canoe, and so on that December day in 1976 I shoved off from the shore to look her over at last, to see just what sort of mess I had gotten myself into.

In just a few paddle strokes the sea smoke rose up and surrounded me, leaving only a winter ocean and a snowy sky. The canoe heavily laden, I felt like a voyageur, one of the early traders who with their frail birchbarks penetrated the North American wilderness. I paddled and the wind grew stronger, biting into the band of flesh between beard and cap. But I could only look away, paddle through the slush, and hope the wind would ease, that vision would return. Instead it grew still stronger, making paddling difficult and bringing harsh spits of fresh snow, and I thought of giving up.

Then, like a wraith, Amaretto appeared out of the snow and gloom before me. She seemed immense just then, a gray wall rising from the dark, smoking water. Alone, bearded with saltwater ice, moored with an iron chain, she was a thoroughbred of a workboat, a sleek seventy-foot double-ender, a stiletto, built in 1918 and worked fifty years at a single task—loading and carrying herring along the ironbound Maine coast.

Then the vast stocks of herring disappeared, many canneries closed up, and Amaretto ended up here—unpainted, neglected, her future uncertain.

I went alongside at last, hefted up the heavy toolboxes, and climbed up to her snowy deck. Drifted and sculpted smooth by the wind, her graceful curve was broken only by a tiny pilothouse aft and fo'c's'le hatch forward. I went forward to the very tip of her bow to look back at her slender shape, a legacy from the time when engines were inefficient beasts and speed came from long, narrow hulls.

But my main interest was in the pilothouse and the engine beneath, to see if it could be started in such weather, or if it was frozen solid, rusted up, useless.

Inside, the dim light from snow-blasted windows showed a tattered chart on a filthy bunk, an out-of-date tidebook by an ancient compass. From below came the musty smell of long-closed spaces.

When I climbed down and saw the engine, my heart sank. It was a rusted monster, easily ten feet long, thirty or forty years old at least. Only the big bank of batteries looked relatively new, and on them and that heap of cast iron rested my hopes for moving the boat to a wharf somewhere before the harbor froze.

I took a three-foot wrench with a four-foot piece of pipe over its handle and put it on the main shaft of the engine. I stepped, then jumped on it. Nothing. The shaft wouldn't budge. Hoping it was just a frozen cooling system, I dug out the propane torch and played its puny flame over the whole engine, concentrating on the pipes and the pumps and the block, hoping to warm the oil and melt the ice.

And as I worked in the dim light of that long-closed space, moving the tiny flame of the torch back and forth, with nothing but the creak of the mooring chain and the moan of the wind outside, the engine came to seem like some prehistoric monster and the torch a sputtering candle held by a pagan priest in an obscure and sinister rite.

Yet when the torch died, used up, empty, I put the big wrench to the shaft again and it moved! So I screwed in another gas cylinder and played its flame over the engine until it too was exhausted.

Then I began to feel the cold again, piercing keenly through insulated coveralls and woollies. But I had come to find out if the old BUDA would start, and I wouldn't quit until I knew. The seller had told me that the batteries were good and that it was a going machine, and that day would surely be the test.

"All of my hopes and most of my fortune lay on that mooring in a harbor fifty miles away."

I cleaned the fuel filters, sprayed starting fluid into the air intake, and tried the starter button.

Nothing. I scraped the battery terminals, checked the connections, and tried again.

Sometimes our hopes get totally wrapped up with a project that seems so big at the time and so small later on. I know mine were, that icy day in that dark engine room, wanting so much for that big engine to start, needing some reassurance that what I was doing wasn't totally hopeless.

And then the starter clunked in, and the huge flywheel turned over slowly, complainingly, once. Then, backfiring smoke and flames from the air intake, echoing horribly in that confined space, it fired up!

Only the starting fluid kept it going—the big BUDA diesel knocked viciously and threatened to quit whenever I slowed the constant spray of ether. The fuel in the lines and the fuel pump had probably turned to jelly in the cold, but still, it ran. And if it would run on starting fluid, it would probably run on diesel. Finally there came the acrid smell of rubber burning, and I looked to find belts turning against the frozen bilge pump, so I let it die.

There was a new sound then with the engine dead—the wind, like a living thing, angry, loud, rattling the doors and windows of the pilothouse, shaking the boat in its fury—and I thought of the canoe and the empty harbor outside, the paddle to shore. The light was dimmer, the short day ending, and it was time to go.

Outside, the afternoon was very different from a few hours before. The wind had come on strong and northeast, the winter storm quadrant. The tops were blowing off the seas outside the harbor, and the boat rose and fell heavily in the swell. From the bow, over the wind, I could hear the chain complaining in the hawsepipe and creaking against the mooring bitts.

Leaning into the wind and the blowing snow, I went forward to check the chain and looked long and hard at the harbor and the shore.

Here and there, behind curtains and drapes pulled against the storm, welcome lights were beginning to come on. I wondered if anyone had noticed me out there at all.

The gusts came stronger, gaining in power and violence, stretching the mooring chain tight and testing all the links, and astern, bobbing in the mean chop, the canoe seemed but a frail cockle. My trip ashore would not be easy.

But a bitter northeaster was surely coming; the signs were plain for all to see. I was already shivering all over; to stay was surely to freeze. The shore lights beckoned and there was no choice but to go.

Kneeling in slush, shipping water constantly, crabbing downwind despite my best efforts with the paddle, I made the shore 200 yards from where I had aimed. From out of the driving snow Cornwallis, my dog, appeared, frantically glad to see me, jumping up and down, barking madly, and shivering violently all at the same time. I hugged him close, then hunched over and put the canoe on my back. Whirled this way and that like a weathervane by the wind, we made our way up the frozen shore, stowed the canoe by a shuttered-up summer cottage, and climbed into my truck beneath the trees.

8

The short day fled before the storm. Our headlights carved a tunnel in black night and white snow. At the edge of vision, shapes of houses slipped past—dim lights in windows, smoke torn from gaunt chimneys. The snow came harder, blowing across the fields, obscuring the road, and in fifty long miles, we met but four other vehicles.

When at last we stopped and got out beside a lightless house, the storm assaulted us with its power. Trees creaked and complained in the woods. The ocean, close at hand, roared dully through the snow. When I found the flashlight, its beam was swirling snow, drifting and piling against the house and its screen porch of piled firewood.

In that rambling and uninsulated farmhouse, my dog and I lived in just two rooms—the kitchen and the room with the woodstove. Inside, my breath was white, the stove cool, the morning's fire barely coals. I put the kindling to it and then the oak, and next it was feed the dog and warm some leftovers. Finally I could sit, pull off my parka and coveralls, put a shot of rum in a hot mug of tea, and feel the incredibly welcome heat of the fire.

On the radio a soothing voice began the tale of Mr. Toad, Badger, and Mole and Ratty, and all their adventures in *The Wind In The Willows*.

"There is nothing as much fun, or simply just as satisfying," the little voice was saying, "as simply messing about in boats."

And outside, even over the radio, I could hear the wind again, working the house, finding its way in through the cracks, around the windows, between the clapboards, moving the curtains.

I thought of the icy water and the tippy canoe and the lonely harbor and wondered if Ratty or Mr. Toad would find that fun.

Another rum burned down my throat. The fire roared in the stove, the sides glowing red here and there. A violent gust of wind shook the house and Cornwallis settled against my leg.

It was the dream of practising the dying art of fish trapping that had brought me to that empty house by those lonely woods. A fish trap is a simple box of net anchored in the water. The fish follow a long leader out from the shore, enter the net through a narrow slot, and are unable to get out—a simple maze for simpler minds.

I wanted to build such a thing of net, line, weights, and buoys, and find a wild, outer island, set the trap, run the leader. I would tent ashore, tend a garden, check the trap every day, and wait for the run of mackerel, making my season in a few weeks of night-and-day work.

By chance, in the fishing village of South Bristol, I met Junior Farrin, a fish trapper, one of the last ones left, and I told him of my dream.

That kind older man encouraged me. He told me that those things were possible, and he said he'd help, showing me how to build, rig, and set out a fish trap.

Then by chance I found Amaretto, the boat that was to drag me so unexpectedly into a time, a place, an occupation so totally different from any I had known before. If I had known then the heartache, the physical pain, the money I would spend and borrow before she was ready, I would have bought a

9

used forty-footer. Something without history or a soul, just some old slab with a lot of good years left, instead of a neglected ghost from another age.

But there was a power in that old boat, something that drew me to her and made me want to make her into the graceful craft I knew she could again become.

When I had at last bought her, my urgent goal of finding a berth—anywhere within fifty miles of South Bristol where I could tie her up to a dock and begin the big refit—gave way to the realities of simply surviving in an uninsulated house. Another northeaster slammed into the coast, and for weeks on end the cold was an iron fist on the land. Our daily routine quickly centered around the woodstove and the woodpile. Getting the truck started, taking a trip into town for groceries, or looking for a berth for the boat became a full day's job.

The winter was the worst in a decade, I was told. Harbors, ice-free for years, skinned, then froze over solid.

The dog and I lived alone, and at night the wind would shake the house, claw at the shutters, filter around the windows. I fed the woodstove, but even glowing cherry-red in places, it would barely keep the cold at bay.

And the time and the loneliness ate at me—so much to do on the boat and unable even to start. A tiny and remote town where I knew few people, the hardest winter in a decade, and always the worries: could I put Amaretto back together, and could I make fish trapping pay?

Once, after two particularly bitter cold weeks, I drove the fifty miles north to try and get out to Amaretto and check on things. I found her decks scoured clean of snow by the wind, the mooring chain pressed a full inch into the iron-hard oak bitts. And below, everything—engine, bilges—frozen solid.

And the forecast "light northerlies" turned instead to an easterly gale in the short time I was aboard, and when I made the shore at last, the canoe held half a foot of water and I was soaked from the hips down.

When I finally got back to South Bristol and dry clothes, my body was warmed up, but my spirits were beaten down. I took Cornwallis down a lane in the woods and out onto the saltwater ice. I needed to walk, to throw sticks for him.

The snow was hip deep along the shore, but out in the middle the ice was hard and bare, blown clean by the wind. It was an arm of the sea, almost landlocked, one mile by three, and Cornwallis ran and ran until he was only a dot disappearing off into the distance. Then he would turn around at last and run back toward me, growing larger, sprouting legs, a tail, and ears, then pass me at full speed to disappear in the other direction.

The light went from the sky and the winter night came on, cold, windy, and dark. Along that frozen shore, there was no house or light, just line after line of dark and silent trees.

We could have been far in the Canadian north, close to the treeline on one of a thousand nameless lakes, hundreds of miles from the nearest human or settlement.

We walked and the tide turned and began to go out beneath us, and as the ice sheet settled with it, it cracked and creaked and moaned and shuddered,

Amaretto, as Muriel, in more prosperous times. (E.L. Boutilier photo)

11

strange, ominous sounds, and Cornwallis stopped his running to hang close by my side, fearful, listening.

And when we were headed back, in the woods again, there was only the faintest starlight through racing clouds to guide us. At last home, in front of the cozy fire, our lights shining out on another wild and bitter night, the feeling of joy and contentedness, just from that walk, that house, that fire, filled me up.

I had all but given up hope of finding a secure place to tie Amaretto, when my friend Junior, the fish trapper who had so encouraged me, asked why I didn't bring her right to his dock in town and work on her there. We looked at the spot together and it was perfect—sheltered from the tide and the main flow of the ice, and just a mile from my house.

A few hours' steam on a winter ocean, and I could breathe easy, have the boat close and begin the big refit. But somehow, with the bay and ocean white outside the harbor day after day and the cold winds shaking the house at night, that little trip grew to seem like an impossible journey, and all of my hopes and most of my fortune lay on that mooring in a harbor fifty miles away.

Thirty days passed. The temperatures seldom got out of the single numbers, and the wind never let up.

Yet even in that frustrating, endless winter, wanting so much to begin the boatwork and still unable to move her because of the weather, there was a kind of grace, a pattern to our lives there in that remote village, in the small things of the day that brought us contentment.

Morning with a hot fire in the stove, listening to the radio at breakfast and watching the day come across the land and the water through frost-laced windows. A walk through the woods to town, past dories and piles of snow-covered lobster traps. Sitting in the one-room general store, nursing a coffee and listening to the drone of the old men speaking of the fishing, stories I had heard before and would hear again and again. Powerful, almost mythical stories of great schools of herring caught or lost. Or stories of the hard winters past, of '36 and '38, when the ocean itself froze out to the islands, eleven miles offshore, and the foolhardy drove their cars across, and all up and down the coast the steamers couldn't land and the passengers had to walk out over the saltwater ice far from shore to get aboard.

And when at last we'd slip out, walk back in the cold, snowy dusk, happy to make it to our own house, it was good and it was enough.

Then, on toward the end of February, there was a break in the weather. A couple of twenty-degree days in a row made it seem positively balmy, and a week of big tides broke up the ice along the shore. I went out to Amaretto and Mr. BUDA spoke for six long hours in his deep-throated voice, and I went through the charts, checked over the steering and running gear, and with the pilothouse heating up from the exhaust pipe and the steady beat of the engine, Amaretto even seemed like a boat again.

And one pale dawn I drove north with a friend to bring her down to Junior's. But then, with the canoe already in the water, a stiff breeze came up from the north, the sun veiled over, and my courage evaporated, just like that. I called it off and we hauled the canoe back onto the shore.

Probably we could have made it. Thirty miles was hardly far. But the combination of the old boat, no skiff or radio, and the violent, unpredictable weather made me nervous. My friend said nothing, but I sensed he thought me overcautious. Probably he had never been caught by a wind on a winter ocean, with no place to go. I had once; it made me cautious forever.

Finally, in the briefest of breaks between violent weather systems, I nursed Amaretto across the restless winter ocean to lie at Junior's wharf.

My friend caught a ride home while I stayed aboard to shut off and wipe down the big engine, pump the bilge, and check the lines, and as Corn and I walked home in the failing light, I was struck by the powerful beauty of the place just then—the silent, tiny harbor, the winter evening, my boat at the wharf. And through the snow, which had begun to fall softly again, came clearly the sound of the horn at Pemaquid, around the point.

The journey that had loomed so large in my mind for so long turned out to be an uneventful, even peaceful one.

And Amaretto, if such a thing can be felt, had seemed eager to be off, to begin her new life, after being so long chained to that granite block in that windy harbor.

The next day came with scudding snow clouds, dark sea, and wind: the lull between storms had lasted long enough to move Amaretto and not a single day more.

Our first job was a deeper berth, for Amaretto's stern was on the bottom every time the tide went out. I rigged shore lines, started up, and dredged us a deeper slip with the wash from the big propeller, a history of the dock and the village excavated layer by layer and blown out behind.

On the shore a few men in heavy pants and wool shirts stood watching. In winter, in a village whose life centers around the small harbor, the arrival of any new boat is news.

When I was done at last and Amaretto lay in a berth of her own making, I walked up the snow-swept wharf and across a little parking lot to Ralph Gray's General Store. In a cleared space among the shelves of gloves, paints, clothes, and hardware was a kerosene heater, and some of the older fishermen of that remote Maine coast village were gathered around. Ralph had a grill and a couple of those old light-green and chrome Hamilton Beach shake mixers, but it was the coffee that I came for. He rinsed out one of the chipped, thick white mugs and poured me a cup.

Outside a snow squall swept down on the harbor, and the boats on their moorings disappeared into the snow, reappearing a few minutes later. After a while one of the younger men turned to me:

"She's the old Muriel, ain't she?"

I nodded.

"Thought so."

On chairs beneath the rows of shelves right up to the ceiling were others—lobstercatchers, draggermen, herring chasers—watching out the windows and listening to us.

"What'cha gonna do with her?"

13

"Haul fish, I guess, build a trap. . . ."

The man nodded, seemed satisfied with my answer.

Then an older man spoke with a gravelly voice. In his early seventies, he was well known in those parts as one whose fishing experience encompassed the dory schooners, the mackerel years, the sailing smacks, and almost every other fishery on this coast since the turn of the century.

"We loaded that boat a time or two." He smiled at the recollection, speaking mostly to himself. "And my dad loaded her with his gang before me. . . ."

"She was a fast one, that Muriel." A third man spoke, and there was a general murmur of assent.

They pretty much forgot about me after that, but the talk went on about Muriel, and of others that I had never heard of but which they had all worked and loaded—the Kingfisher, the Mary Ann, the Jacob Pike and the Pauline, the Nereid and the Bofisco.

And of where the herring had been that year, who caught them and how, and other details and stories that after a while all seemed to merge into one.

Amaretto first slid into the salt water at the Hodgdon Brothers yard in East Boothbay, just across the river from the store where we warmed ourselves. It was 1918 and the war was on, and she was built for a sardine cannery in North Lubec, Maine, far to the east and north and just across a bay from Canada, one of the most remote canneries in the state. Named for the younger sister of one of the owners, she was the pride of the cannery and of the little community that was built around it.

This was a herring coast in those days, and a fleet of boats like Amaretto worked its entire length. In the warm months the herring, schools of 5-, 6-, and 7-inch fish, would move in from the deep ocean water and "strike the shore." And when and where they did the men waited with weirs or traps, leading the fish with long lines of spruce boughs and poles driven into the mud. In other places they would wait with nets in dories, and when the fish swam into a shallow cove, they would set a net across the mouth to "shut it off" and capture the fish that way. Sometimes in a single cove the men would shut off thousands of bushels of herring, enough to load many boats like mine, and their season would be made.

It was a remote coast, too. The roads leading down all those peninsulas were dirt tracks, impassable in any but dry or frozen weather. All news, freight, and supplies came by steamer. On the outer islands and in the remote fish camps inhabited only in the summertime, boats such as Amaretto were often about the only contact with civilization, bringing news of the world as well as groceries, and taking out the fish. Lobstering wasn't a shadow of the business it is now, and for many, it was the herring that paid the bills.

The day began to go from the sky outside the frosted windows, and Cornwallis gave me the "home" look from his little corner by the door. I stood up, nodded to the men, and Corn and I walked out together into the snowy dusk.

And as we walked up the road, I remember feeling that at last the project could begin.

Then the winter closed in once again with a vengeance. Northeast gales battered the coast with snow and violent winds and high tides.

Sometimes at night, when the wind clawed around the eaves of that old house and the snow hissed against the windows, the fears and the doubts would come again. I'd lie awake feeling sure that what I wanted to do with the boat, with trapping, was impossible.

"Amaretto's too old," the voice would say, or, "The money won't be near enough," or, "Fish trapping will never work out." The "what ifs" would spin round and round, and sleep came hard.

But then at last the pink would come to the sky above the iced-over bay and fields and forests outside. I'd stick my head out of the sleeping bag, see my

"If there was a bright spot in my life then, it was Cornwallis, a good and true friend."

15

breath white before me, then quick, pull on some clothes and build a fire. Cornwallis would stretch and get up, and we'd both stand by the woodstove as the fire roared and the sides glowed dull red.

I'd eat a hot breakfast, put some lunch in a bag, pull on insulated coveralls, hat, and gloves, and step out into the crisp air to walk through the snowy woods down to the harbor and begin another day.

There were immense jobs crying for my attention—the engine room, the plumbing, the wiring. But at zero or five degrees, my hands only froze to the tools. The only place where work was possible was in the fo'c's'le, where there was a little woodstove to take the sting out of the cold. So each morning I'd carry Cornwallis down the ladder to the boat, brush the fresh snow from the fo'c's'le hatch, help him down that ladder, light a fire in the woodstove, and get to work.

The pieces of the old—the shelves and benches, the tired, broken table—I fed into the stove, and the new I shaped from oak and maple and cherry planks.

In the depth of that awful winter, with loneliness and money worries eating away at me, time in the fo'c's'le with the dog asleep, music on the radio, and the wild world outside was what I needed.

I saved the porcelain sink and brass faucets and gave them a new home in a maple counter with cherry-faced shelves.

Now and again a particularly powerful gust would heel the boat over at the wharf, and I could hear the moan of the wind even over the radio and the tools.

While Cornwallis slept I built an oak galley table, with shelves and drawers for storage. While I sanded, sawed, and drilled, he'd sleep, roll over, and sleep some more.

The walls, the inner skin or "ceiling" of the boat, turned out to be beautiful long-leafed southern yellow pine. I scraped off half a dozen layers of paint, sanded it, and gave it a simple linseed oil finish, until it shone, giving the once dingy fo'c's'le a warm, cozy feeling.

It was foolish, I supposed, to spend so much time on the fo'c's'le, but I knew that the job in the months to come would be frustrating, dirty, thankless work, and the value of a single clean and graceful place to retreat to would be high.

Sometimes I'd give up my work for a bit and go over to the store for a mug-up.

One bitter day when only the masts of the boats could be seen above the arctic sea smoke in the harbor, the men spoke of a place called Seal Island and a man named David. It was a wild and a lonely place, they said, one of the outermost islands, a little-visited ridge of rock and wild grass, the last of the land before it plunged to the lightless depths offshore. But there was something about the place—it attracted the herring, somehow; there were often fish there when they were nowhere else on the coast.

David was a herring fisherman from Vinalhaven, another island. Seal Island was his second home; night after night he searched and waited for the herring around that bleak and lost spot.

He had powers, they said, to find herring when no one else could.

And often the men would forget about me and talk about where they had seen Amaretto, and who had her then, and where the fish were, and who had caught them.

And seated by that cozy stove, instead of seeing a tired boat with a broken-down engine I'd envision Amaretto as she might be, freshly painted, her engine, wiring, and plumbing renewed. I'd believe that perhaps there was magic, power, and mystery, after all, in that business I seemed to be drifting into.

Each evening with another little job done—a counter, a shelf finished, the dust and chips swept up—I'd slide back the hatch cover, and Cornwallis and I would look out and find our tracks obliterated, the deck drifted over with fresh snow. I'd pull my hat down and my collar up, and we'd step out into a world of fading light, windblown harbor, and empty, snow-swept road.

The bitter weather kept on, week after week without a break. When I tried to work in the engine room my hands would freeze to the tools. When I wanted to go to a nearby town to get some parts, my truck refused to start. Finally we took just to walking through the woods to work, building in the fo'c's'le until the weather broke.

If there was a bright spot in my life then, it was Cornwallis, a good and true friend. Every third day at least I'd try to quit early, take a long walk with him out on the saltwater ice or through the deep snow, down one of the roads back to deserted summer cottages, throwing things for him again and again, trying to push back the walls I felt closing around me.

One of those early March days there was a bump alongside, and I pushed back the hatch to see the red morning sky's promise fulfilled: the sky and the water were dark and snow was flying with the wind, driving the little fleet from around the corner in New Harbor to lie beside us, where there was more shelter.

So I gave it up early and walked home, with head down against the snow and wind, Cornwallis close behind. The road home seemed especially long and cold and dark, and as I trudged through the cold to a lightless, chill, and silent house, the winter seemed endless, the project at hand, immense. I felt that that old boat and my idea of fish trapping were impossible, the products of an unstable mind, of a habit of jumping into things before clearly thinking them through. The refit would obviously be more expensive than I had figured. There might not be enough money left over to buy a fish trap, and even if there was, I didn't know if I could make one work.

But most of all it was the short bitter days and the long dark nights, the empty house, the lack of friends that wore me down.

There were things I should have been doing those long winter evenings— making lists, laying out the work ahead, even just reading—but I had little strength or desire for other than simple meals, cleaning up, lying next to the woodstove and Cornwallis, and drinking hot rums.

How to describe those dreary, windy March afternoons when it seems as if winter will never ever come to an end? I worked in the fo'c's'le and now and again would put down my tools and listen to the wind, howling outside,

"The winter seemed endless, the project at hand, immense."

18

humming in the rigging, making the whole boat resonate, drowning out the radio at times.

The sixth of April brought a westerly gale, cold and violent all day out of a clear sky—mast and rigging resonating, shaking the whole boat. I tried my damndest but could not stop it. Two days later came a southeast gale with driving snow that switched to northerly in the afternoon, very strong and very cold. I gave it up early to sit by the fire at home and do some paperwork.

Then one afternoon I was splitting wood and stopped and heard for the first time the sound of water running beneath the deep snow.

Two weeks later an afternoon came warm and fair, and when Cornwallis and I walked back together through the woods, the bogs and the low places were all full of the peepers, small tree frogs, singing their little song, and it was a welcome, welcome sound.

The longer days and softer weather gave me courage to start the worst project of all—taking the old monster of an engine to pieces, ripping out the floor and the roof of the pilothouse to get ready to hoist it all out with a crane.

I started Mr. BUDA up for the last time, poured a gallon of oil into the air intake to coat everything, patted the valve covers for thirty years' loyal service, and then began to take it apart piece by piece. I hoped, I really did, that someone would come along and buy her, get her running again, but I suspected that it was the end.

Each night I'd come home covered with black grease and dirty oil from my feet to the very roots of my hair.

One day just when things were at their very worst, their filthiest and most discouraging, a stranger up on the wharf called down to say that he had worked on the Muriel years ago, and that I had gotten myself one good boat.

On a mid-April afternoon, with the daffodils just showing on the south sides of the houses in the village, an old friend came from all the way across the country to work with Cornwallis and me. By train and by bus, the very last lap down the peninsula by thumb, Ann brought a bag of clothes, another of books, and a stoppered bottle of Pacific water for Amaretto. She said that nursing school started in the fall, and she needed a good-paying summer job.

I hoped she wasn't easily discouraged. If there was grace, beauty, or romance in it all—the unheated farmhouse, the old boat, the New England fishing village—it was lost on me. I just got up each morning and headed out the door to the boat before the sun was up. On few days was any progress visible at all. On some, working in the cold, damp, engine room, covered with grease and with rain pelting against the pilothouse and dripping down through the deck onto my tools and me, it seemed as if the whole project was going backward.

Fish trapping was a venture gone by, at least for that year, and with Ann, I had to be brutally honest: the whole project was on the shakiest of grounds, and the chances of finishing the boat with the money at hand were slim at best. The chances of buying a fish trap were none. What we would do with the boat if we got it done was even less clear, and for the moment there wasn't money for rent, food, the boat, and to pay her too.

"That's OK," she said. "I can't go anywhere anyway. I've spent all my money just getting here." She looked outside the windows at the evening light slanting

"On few days was any progress visible at all."

across the brown fields and on the bay beyond, tilting her head for a moment to listen to the sweet sound of the peepers coming through the screens.

"And besides, I've always wanted to see Maine."

She set to work with enormous energy, scraping and painting the hull, caulking the decks, cleaning out the fo'c's'le, doing all the precise detail work that I never had time for. In a few weeks, she had Amaretto looking like that graceful boat I had dreamed she could be.

And after half a winter of looking for an engine I could afford, I found a war surplus Gray Marine 6-71, the father of the modern high-speed diesel.

It had come out of a landing craft somewhere, for on the side of the governor, clearly marked, was the "BATTLE" notch. It was for use when the sky rained fire and hot steel and the boat was full of frightened men, crouched low with rifles and full packs; when just a few extra rpm's might make the difference between victory and death, and if the engine had to be scrapped or rebuilt afterwards was of no importance.

I won't dwell on the heavy reduction and reverse gear I had to air freight from Seattle. Or the power take-off or the hydraulic system, each expensive and requiring extensive modifications to fit the 1942 Gray Marine.

I assembled this vintage old-and-new collection into a power plant on the floor of the local engine dealer's shop. He would have far preferred to have sold me a new $20,000 engine, and his disappointment came out in constant disparaging remarks about the mess on his floor. Time and time again I had to say to myself, like a litany, "This is a good machine. I know I can make it work."

Winter still seemed endless. Spring was struggling to come, and it was a hard and lean time for us. From my journal:

April 26 — Cold and mean, a gale from the east, and steady slanting rain. In less than a month we have to move aboard, and still the boat is a shambles from bow to stern. The decks leak over the fo'c's'le, the new engine is still up in the shop needing flywheel, reverse gear, power take-off, another oil pan, and who knows what else that I can't afford.

So cleaned things up a bit and tried to examine my doubts and worries and discouragement, to try and see some hope, some light at the end of the tunnel in this whole project, but found none.

Then on a May afternoon, the crane gang at the shipyard lowered the old/ new Gray Marine through the gutted pilothouse for a perfect fit onto the remade engine beds. And so began the transformation of Amaretto from an engineless ugly duckling, high in the water, into a sardine carrier as sleek and as graceful as those we had begun to see traveling up and down the coast, looking for herring.

Ann went home early, for we had to be ready to move out of the house in a few days, and I stayed late to finish up the wiring in the fo'c's'le. When I headed up the road for home, it was pretty much dark, but I could see across the river to the lights of East Boothbay, the village where Amaretto had been built so many years ago.

With the engine together and in the boat at last, a great weight seemed to have been lifted from my shoulders. I had already started it up in the shop, and it ran well. The future was no less uncertain—we were almost out of money, with a lot still to do—but somehow I felt as if the worst was over.

Then as I looked out and across the river again, in my mind's eye, the scene changed: the lights were kerosene, the trees smaller, the buildings newer. And there on the launching ways, shining in the moonlight of a May evening, was the Muriel. It was 1918, and she was all fresh painted, waiting for the morning, to kiss the salt water for the first time, steam to the east, and begin.

Our bank account wound down toward zero. I called around to all the sardine companies to see if they needed an extra boat for the season, but no one did.

All dressed up with no place to go, we moved aboard that first week of June. Ann had made covers for the long seat cushions, put up photos, put flowers on the galley table, made the fo'c's'le into an incredibly cozy and inviting place. But I didn't know where we were headed, or what we were going to do. "Something'll probably come up, it usually does," I always said confidently, hiding my fears and doubts.

It became harder and harder for me to get my wallet out or write a check.

Meals began to appear on the table down in the fo'c's'le without my paying for them. There would be mussels and clams from Ann's trips in the skiff with Cornwallis, foraging at low tide. Junior Farrin brought rhubarb from his garden and mackerel from his fish trap.

The people from the village dropped food by: lobsters, fish, early garden produce. They wanted to see Amaretto working again, and helped us in any way they could.

Once, when I was at my wit's end trying to find a different oil pan so that I could mate a 1942 engine to a 1964 power take-off, an older man with a limp stopped by the boat and asked me up to his house. There, in a musty room with varnished fir wainscoting, were crates and crates of parts for my engine—still in their original boxes, wrapped in waxed paper and Cosmoline. An oil pan, just what I had been looking for, new injectors, a spare raw water pump. I felt like a kid in a toy store.

"Take what you want," he said, "pay me when you can. I had a dragger for years with one of those old Gray Marine 6-71's in it."

I went through the treasures on the floor and he looked out the window. The view was to the river below, and Amaretto's bow could just be seen.

"When I was a boy, my dad was loading the old Muriel, and I was out on the twine with him, helpin' the men out. When the skipper had his trip, he asked my dad and me aboard for a turn down the bay. It was my first time aboard such a big boat, and when they got clear of the twine and down through the ledges, the skipper set a deck bucket down behind the wheel for me.

"'Here, boy, steer a spell if you've a mind to it,' he said. I could barely see over the compass, but he and my dad had a nip, and now and again my dad would give the wheel a few spokes to keep us headed right. . . .

"A turn down the bay."

"That was 1923, and old Monty had 'er then. Oh, wasn't she a sight. Kept her like a yacht, old Monty did.

"'C'mon, boy, Muriel's comin' in fer a trip. We better nip over and get a look at her. . . . Not too many like her around. . . .' Dad'd get me up early whenever she came into the river for a trip o' fish, and if it came right for 'em, Monty and my dad'd slip off for a turn down the bay and there'd be the deck bucket behind the big wheel for me when we cleared the ledges. . . ."

His voice trailed off. Neither of us said anything for a long while. Then he sighed, "So it was a surprise for all of us here when she showed up in the harbor, at Junior's wharf, out of the blue like that. We thought she was gone, thought she'd lie on the mooring until the life was out of 'er, fit to be towed up some slough and left to die. . . ."

He turned around, waved at the pile of parts scattered around the room. "So take what you need. . . . You're doin' something, puttin' that lady back together."

Three

On a black and cool May evening, Junior took me out with him and showed me, in just the briefest encounter, what it was about herring that made the fishery seem so mysterious, so different from any other that I knew.

Only the week before, the herring had arrived on the coast, and a change had come over the harbor.

Each evening, after the lobstercatchers had all come in and the harbor was still, there would be a burst of activity. Pickups would rattle down to the shore, men would get into their outboards or lobsterboats and cruise slowly out of the harbor, looking, sometimes towing dories full of net behind. A faraway drone would become a plane, flying lazily along that deeply indented coast, banking over each cove and little inlet in turn, looking for fish.

In the breezy dusk, Junior stopped by Amaretto and asked me to go on his rounds with him, the nightly check of his coves. We motored in and out of a dozen coves in his sixteen-foot outboard, equipped with only the simplest depth sounder, a "flasher." There were dories full of net or twine in some of the coves, and Junior dropped me off to pump them out while he looked for fish with the depth finder.

As I pumped and it grew dark, I looked up the bay behind us and made out the shapes of other small boats like ours, cruising the far shores, looking.

Junior picked me up, and as we motored to the next cove, he spoke of the herring.

"We used the pole before we had these sounders," he said, showing me the sounding pole. Some ten or twelve feet long, flattened at one end like an oar, it was unlike anything I had seen before.

"If there's a good bunch of fish, you can just shove the pole down into the water and feel 'em. . . ." He thrust the pole vertically into the water beside the boat as we lay stopped in one of the coves. He held the very tip of the pole lightly in his fingers: "Sometimes you can even tell how big they are by the way their noses bump the pole. . . ."

But the coves were quiet, the sounder dark.

"How come these are 'your' coves, and Henry Jones has all the ones that way?" I pointed back toward the coves on the other side of the bay, for I had noticed each of the three groups of herring fishermen out of the harbor seemed to have their "own" coves to tend.

"Tradition. . . ." Junior shrugged. "My dad tended these coves when I was a boy, and I guess Henry's dad tended those coves. . . ."

Then at the very last stop, Christmas Cove, with the night in the sky, we found them.

Junior had dropped me off to pump rainwater out of a string of dories. There was a cool breeze off the river, and I wished I had brought something warmer to wear.

Then I saw it—a dim light, moving, restless, pulsing, deep in the black water. It was unlike anything I had ever seen before, and as I watched it, I could feel the goose bumps rising on my back. Finally I put down the pump and realized what it was—phosphorescence, stirred up by a school of herring.

Junior saw it too and cruised over the spot with the skiff. I could see the depth finder light up with the fish.

And I understood then what it was about this fishery that made it so different from any other I had been in—there was an intense relationship between hunter and prey. Junior was in the skiff, the fish were out in the deeper water, yet I sensed they were like two wary creatures, each circling, taking measure of the other.

In the dory in which I sat was a pile of twine, a wall of net with corks on the top and leads on the bottom, 1200 feet long. Enough to seal off the mouth of the cove, trapping the fish behind it, until a carrier like Amaretto could come for them.

But the fish first had to enter the cove, for out where they were swimming, the water was too deep for the net to be effective. They would swim beneath it, escape.

It grew fully dark; a damp cold came on. The summer houses around the cove were lightless, boarded up, empty. The warm weather seemed very far away. Still Junior cruised back and forth, watching the fish, waiting for them to make a move shoreward.

I strained my eyes and once again saw the faintest glimmer beneath the surface. It seemed to be further out that time.

Then the fish were gone; we both sensed it.

But Junior still stalked back and forth a long while outside the cove mouth before finally he gave up and the outboard bumped back alongside the dory.

Junior shook his head. "Not coming in tonight. I guess we'll go home," was all he said.

We motored up the river in silence, but when we rounded the point and made South Bristol, I invited him aboard. Ann had lit a fire in the stove and there was music on the radio. I gave him a glass with bourbon in it and Junior looked around at all that we had done, all the little touches, the flowers, the pictures, that made it our home. He smiled, and I could tell he was remembering other times, other people in that fo'c's'le, perhaps even with his dad, when he was just a boy, stopping below for a "nip" with the skipper after they had loaded her with their herring.

He wasn't a man of many words, but he seemed glad at all we had done, glad that Amaretto would be running, working again, instead of just forgotten, chained to that granite mooring.

I asked him about what we had seen that evening, if it was always so frustrating.

"Sometimes," he said, "a big bunch of fish'll hang off a cove all summer, and you'll have to watch every night, sometimes all night, waiting for 'em to come in. It might be the windiest, most rotten night of the year, and if you're there, you'll get 'em. If not. . . ." His voice trailed off.

27

"But if y'get 'em, and everything comes just right, the companies'll send all their boats, and you'll make a season or more in a few days. . . ."

Then he spoke of another island, and of a great school of herring that had come when he was young.

It had been a poor year, he said, with a couple of skinny ones before that. And it was late in the season, with the hard months right around the corner. They'd about given the herring up, were about to put the dories on the bank for the winter, when one of the fishermen steamed into the harbor with word of a big bunch in a cove on one of the outer islands, west of Pemaquid.

Within an hour they all set out, towing their dories full of twine in long lines behind them down the bay.

It was, they realized as soon as they had rounded the corner and could see the fish finning and flipping all across the broad cove, a very great school, one of the biggest seen in years, perhaps fifty boatloads for the biggest sardine carriers.

The cove was no one's—too remote to be "watched" regularly. So the three herring gangs got together and agreed to work with one another, sharing the fish, pooling all their dories and nets to get them.

In an hour it was done. The cove was sealed off, the herring trapped in fifteen or twenty acres of water behind the line of net. The fishermen set the anchors, checked for chafing where the ends of the net came ashore.

"Then he spoke of another island, and of a great school of herring that had come when he was young."

28

It was late in the day by then and they hadn't yet called the canneries. So they all left, taking their boats back across the six miles of water to home. They called the sardine companies and it was all set up—in the morning the canneries would send as many boats as they could. In town that night the men and their families talked about what they would do with the badly needed money.

The next day came stormy, a southeaster, the first real hard blow of the fall. The men looked out rain-slashed windows at the boats sailing back and forth on their moorings, and at the bay, feather white with the wind.

It was the second night before the storm blew itself out, and the day came crisp and clear. Summer turned into fall, just like that.

With high hopes they set out, a parade of boats. On the horizon were a dozen big sardine carriers, the fish plants sending all they had, for the season was late, the pack skinny, the market strong, everything just right, the herring fishermen's dream.

"Just a few days was all we needed, to get all those fish out . . . just one day at least, and we would 'a had some kind of a season. . . ."

"But when we made the island, came around the point, . . . our 'duries were on the beach, all broken up, and the fish were gone. The storm had pooched it all."

For a long while after that, no one spoke. Then he sighed and got up. I climbed up the ladder with him and bade him goodnight. The stars were bright; the wind had come around into the west and freshened.

I called and called, up and down the coast, and still could find no work for Amaretto.

The only chance at all seemed to be hauling herring for lobster bait. On Vinalhaven and other offshore islands, we were told, the fishermen had trouble getting the bait they need. It had to be hauled by truck on the ferries from the mainland, and a boat like this might make a living buying herring and selling it to the fishermen and lobster dealers.

It was said to be a hard, dirty, and cutthroat business. That was it—a rumor that there might be work, if we hustled for the market. It was sketchy, but if there was money in it, we had to go.

I found a banker willing to lend money on a boat older than his dad. The first of June came and went and we were still finishing up. I'd be up until eleven or twelve each night, hooking up the wiring, the hydraulics, all the little odds and ends.

Finally, on a mid-June afternoon, Amaretto backed away from the dock under her own power, and we ran up and down the river for a few warm and troublefree hours, trying the new engine out.

That evening we invited Junior and our other winter-made friends down for beer on the wharf. There were guitars and singing, but best of all was taking them down into the engine room one at a time, completing the starting circuit with a screwdriver—for the wiring was still incomplete—and listening to the sweet sound of that thirty-year-old engine rolling into life. I'd snap the throttle for the crowd on the dock, and we'd drink again to the engine and the season ahead.

With the warm weather, the evenings would bring more and more people wandering down to the wharf to stand there and look down, talking among themselves. And the conversations would drift down to us—of where they had seen Amaretto before, of who was running her then, who had the fish, and on and on, one story flowing into another. It made Ann and me feel proud, ready to burst sometimes, for Amaretto and how far she had come.

So the time approached when we would be off—to exactly what we could not be sure. To have the end and also a beginning so close filled us both with anticipation.

But there was more—some powerful mystery in that herring business that we were about to get into. I felt it that night in the dory with Junior; I felt it watching the plane rise into the western sky every dusk, the silent men leaving the harbor every evening. I had felt it even that winter, when the ocean smoked and the harbor froze, and the men sat in the store and put their backs to the stove. On the wild days when the snow swirled and the wind howled, it seemed always to be the herring they yarned about. The stories would be told over and over again—mythical, powerful tales.

So if for us, fish trapping was not to be, that was OK. For by then we felt caught up in something bigger and far more exciting. It seemed somehow right and proper that Amaretto, or Muriel, should do again what she was built for, even if only for bait.

And on a warm and cloudless June evening, when the last, last things were almost done, another sardine carrier, the Betsy and Sally, slipped up the river, and we lay side by side, both freshly painted and ready for our first fish. Her skipper came aboard Amaretto, and on that perfect evening so full of promise, we toasted our health, our boats, the fish, and whatever the new season might bring.

So finally on a cool morning, with little fanfare, our journey began.

Ann poured the bottle of Pacific water over the bow. I said a little prayer, and the lines were off.

Our friends waved and called out to us, and then the harbor fell astern. The rich, pungent smell of the land gave way to the cool and damp of the sea. We were on our own.

The last of the money was spent on the fuel in the tank. We had to find a way to make her pay.

John's Bay opened up before us, and at Pemaquid Point we met the ocean, the wind, and the fog.

The compass wasn't swung, the radar wasn't tuned, and as we rolled heavily in the trough of the seas, there was the crash of unstowed things falling and a whimper from Cornwallis in the bunk.

Ann stood at the window of the cramped pilothouse. She said little, but her face was drawn, her knuckles white. Our bow disappeared into the swirling gray, and we could hear heavy seas booming against the cliffs close to port and the bellow of a fog signal. The elation of being underway at last was quickly replaced by a dozen cold fears all crowding in on one another. I wanted to go below to check the engine room, but I couldn't leave the wheel.

To make the island before dark would have meant running all day in such conditions, along an unfamiliar and unforgiving coast. My courage wasn't up to it, so when we rounded the point and the horn was on our stern, I turned north, to the islands and back channels of Muscongus Bay, the longer, less direct route. But there the sea might be calmer, the fog thinner.

And in just an hour it was easy, warm, summer again. The fog gave way to shining green shore, trees and cottages, lobster buoys and sailboats. We relaxed, took turns lying out on deck in the sun, and waved to people in little boats.

We passed the narrows at Hog Island, and I began to trust the new engine and its installation—a welcome change after sleepless night upon sleepless night of wondering if I had done this or that thing right.

By Friendship Harbor, in early afternoon, we met the fog again. I trusted the radar and compass well enough by then; we could have gone on, I supposed—made Port Clyde, or Tenants Harbor, maybe even anchored somewhere in the quiet and the solitude of the Muscle Ridge Islands.

But the harbor beckoned so; the desire just to stop, drop the hook, clean up the debris, drink, was overwhelming.

So we did. Ghosting in among the fleet of moored lobsterboats, we found a spot with good water and swinging room. The chain rattled over the bow and all was still.

We sat a while in the engine-warm pilothouse. There was rum, and the thrill of having the boat alive under us at last, of being on our way to wherever we were going. The fog sifted in and out, showing one moment only a gray wall, another, a glimpse of lobsterboats and houses on the shore.

Evening came, and we took the outboard ashore for a walk with the dog. The village seemed deserted; the fog poured around us, the trees, the trim, white houses. From a great distance there came the sound of a foghorn, and we could feel the strain and worry of those first hours falling away.

Then came that feeling, so sudden and strong that it didn't seem to make any sense.

It was in the foggy darkness, with Amaretto materializing dimly ahead, a ghost, a specter in the gloom, swinging back and forth slowly in the tide beneath her shining masthead light, and it was this:

That Amaretto, come back to life now, had a powerful destiny all her own. It had to do somehow with the herring that seemed to be coming back to the coast and with the old ways that had been almost forgotten.

Four

There was a good sea running that first afternoon when we lay off Vinalhaven, trying to figure out the best way in. The island seemed surrounded by a maze of smaller islets and reefs, all breaking and showing their gleaming white teeth. The fog began to sift in thick around us again, and the breeze had begun to pick up.

Our chart was all ripped from being folded too many times in too many hands; the part with the enlargement of the harbor entrance was gone.

The prudent mariner, approaching Vinalhaven under such conditions, would be well advised, if he had no pressing reason to go there, to run off to the east or the west, where there are other, better harbors, with far easier access. But the evening was coming on, and we were exhausted from tedious navigating in and out of fog all day long. Our desire for a harbor was strong.

So with my heart pounding in my throat and the seas breaking heavily on the ledges close around us, we came to Carver's Harbor, Vinalhaven Island.

If there were prosperity in that town where we had come to put together a season, pay the spring's bills and make the winter's money, it was hidden from us that day.

Perched around that natural basin of a harbor were row after row of tired looking but once elegant white frame houses. Along the shore were fish houses—lobstermen's workshops—on granite wharves, and the shells of what must have once been fish plants, vacant and in disrepair.

Gone were the anchored yachts and little sailboats of the mainland harbors, replaced by a businesslike fleet of lobsterboats, seiners, and dories—more than I had seen in any other harbor.

And the place had an aura, a feeling about it that I hadn't ever quite felt before. As we drifted slowly by the ferry wharf, trying to figure out where to tie up, I suddenly had an odd feeling of having stepped back in time. Not long—just a few decades or so.

Then a battered pickup truck bounced to a stop at one of the wharfs, three husky men waved us in, and the spell was broken.

They took our lines, came aboard, and introduced themselves: Jim, Alton, and Tom. One of the men was sipping from something in a paper bag. Jim got right to the point:

"Hello, hello," he said. He was the talkative leader of the group. "You boys lookin' fer a trip 'o fish?"

"Soon as I get squared away, we will be," said I. "You think we could sell some bait in here?"

"Plenty of market. You could sell a boatload in here tomorrow. Plenty of market," he repeated.

Jim was an enthusiastic, optimistic, really likeable sort of guy. He also had a hard time, we learned later, telling anyone anything they didn't want to hear.

33

"If there were prosperity in that town where we had come to put together a season, pay the spring's bills, and make the winter's money, it was hidden from us that day."

34

"How 'bout fish?" I asked. "Any trouble getting what we want?"

"Plenty of fish," Jim repeated, "plenty of market. We'll load you any night 'ya want. . . . "

"Plenty of fish," "plenty of market." I was to remember those words. But for then, believing him, reassured that we had come to the right spot, that at last we might make some desperately needed money, I took a good pull from the paper bag when it came my way again.

We slept well in our new home that night, in that little ocean outpost. Gone were the fears and doubts of would it work, and would there be enough money, replaced by excitement and enthusiasm, immensely more useful feelings.

The first boat started up at four-thirty the next morning, and I slipped out of my pilothouse bunk to see the eastern sky yellow over the harbor, and men oaring out to their boats. "Oaring" was standing up in a tiny punt and paddling with one oar. Rowing seemed to be in disfavor there.

I pulled on jeans and a flannel shirt and carried Cornwallis up the ladder. Together we walked around the harbor to see where the lobsterboats were getting bait.

A lot of the boats were tied up below a long, dirty, white building set on a wharf. I climbed down a ladder to a float where a man was dipping some awful looking stuff out of some wooden tanks into plastic baskets with hundreds of little holes drilled in the sides. A sort of juice ran out of the holes.

What was left in the baskets looked like what a whale might puke up if it swallowed a school of herring that disagreed with him: heads, tails, bodies, eyeballs, all floating in a thick syrup.

"How's your bait holdin' out?" New to this whole business, I didn't know if one took orders, or just showed up with a load and started peddling.

The man finished dipping another basketful before answering.

"That yer boat?" He jerked his head in the general direction of Amaretto.

"Yup."

"You gonna be luggin' bait too?"

I nodded. The man looked me up and down and gave me a queer, almost pitying look before answering.

He said, "That's sure one son-of-a-whore business you're getting into."

"What d'ya mean?"

"Well," he shuffled over to the bait tank and started dipping again, "you'll see. . . ."

"Well, can I sell you some . . . ?"

He shrugged. "Sure, check with me tomorrow. We'll need some by and by. . . ."

I went over to the next place. A bungalow-sized cinder block building sat by the edge of a granite wharf. The wharves are among the most noticeable parts of the Maine coast—built of VW-sized pieces of granite, left over from the turn of the century when granite was the principal trade among many of these rocky islands.

Inside were more wooden bait tanks. Just sticking my head in was enough. The smell made me want to retch. I waited for the man to come outside where there was a little more air.

35

A husky, balding man in a brown, bait-stained shirt dragged a couple of baskets of foul smelling stuff out of the building over to a little elevator platform. He pushed a button on the side of a piling, and the platform slowly descended to a waiting lobsterboat.

"How 'ya doing for bait?" I asked.

The platform stopped level with the lobsterboat. The lobsterman pulled the baskets aboard and dumped all four of them into a big wooden barrel, mixing it with liberal handfuls of what looked like rock salt from a bag.

"Got plenty of brim," the man said, "but we could probably use three, four hundred bushels of herrin', 'n a day or two. . . ."

"What's brim?" I said, almost afraid to ask.

He dragged another couple of full baskets out of the building and jerked his hand toward the loathsome contents. "Brim" was apparently what was left after you cut the fillets off a fish and let the remains stand in the sun a day or two. They had been heavily salted, but there were a few maggots clearly visible.

"Redfish racks," he called them.

I walked back to the boat, slightly less excited about baiting than I had been the night before.

The sun got a little higher, the air warmer. Ann made breakfast and we sat out on the hatch covers in t-shirts, eating and savoring the morning. The last of the lobsterboats disappeared out the harbor mouth, leaving a little fleet of skiffs and punts behind.

"I think we should enjoy this morning," I said.

"I am," said Ann. "It's beautiful."

"I mean, really enjoy it. . . ."

Ann put down her cup and looked at me. "What are you getting at?"

"I mean we shouldn't have any illusions about this business we're getting into."

"What do you mean?"

"I mean, you wouldn't believe the shit they're using for bait. Gaah! It makes me want to puke. Those lobsters can't be too particular about what they eat." I gave her an unabridged description of my travels.

"Not like Alaska, eh?" she said.

I shook my head gloomily. When I had met Ann, she had been in charge of quality control in a small cannery in a remote Alaska village. I operated a sixty-foot boat for the cannery, buying fish from fishermen in dozens of lonely bays and fiords, far from any town. We got our fish when they were but a few hours out of the water, weighed them, and put them directly into ice water.

It was a clean business.

"Well, I don't think we can afford to be too particular about how we make money," said Ann, her gaze deliberately fixed on the harbor, the morning. "And it *is* a beautiful spot. . . ."

We spent much of the day building a "sock brailer" to load our fish aboard. Most of the other sardine carriers along the coast used a so-called fish pump to accomplish this task—essentially, a big hose attached to a very large pump down in the engine room. When enough fish were concentrated in the net, the hose would be used to suck the fish out of the net, through the pump, and into a "dewatering box," a series of screens that separated the water from the fish. Fish pumps were expensive, however; to save money, we elected to try a sock brailer. This was a long tube of net with a hoop at either end. One hoop was tied into our fish hold, the other attached to a long handle, like a dipnet. The way it was supposed to work is that we'd come alongside a netful of fish and swing our boom out; then, using our winch to lift and my back to push the handle into the fish, we'd dip the hoop in and hoist it back up again. The fish would theoretically slide along the net and into the fish hold, without our having to swing the boom back and forth with each hoist.

Evening brought a party, at a farmhouse filled with a dozen husky strangers, all herring fishermen. "Mexican night": a salute to our neighbors to the south, but mostly to their drink—cheap tequila. My head spun from the tequila, my stomach burned from Mexican food.

"Hey, c'mon, I'll take you flying, show you around." A wiry stranger shook my shoulder. I looked around and saw that Ann was surrounded by men, evidently enjoying herself.

So in a moment we were in a pickup, bouncing down a dirt road, the dust swirling up behind us. A mongrel dog barked in the back, leaning into the turns, his ears trailing downwind.

"Yeah, wait 'til you get in the air . . . you'll get a better idea of the lay of the land," the young pilot yelled over the noise of the truck as we drove. "I fly 'bout every night when there's fish around."

We stopped by a sagging barn. Beyond was a field of tall grass, with thick woods crowding in on three sides. We rolled out a tiny red antique of a plane. Dave, the pilot, waved me into the seat. "Stand on those pedals," he said, and before I had even had time for a good look around, he had rocked the engine into life, and we were bumping along the mowed strip that was the runway. The dog chased along, barking under the wingtip.

The plane seemed more like a big kid's model or something from the Smithsonian than a real plane. For controls the little two-seater had a stick, rudder pedals, flap lever, choke and throttle, and trim wheel. That was about it. The "electronics package" was a little walkie-talkie whose antenna Dave could stick out the window when he talked.

He put the throttle forward, the grass slid by, the tail wheel was up, and we bounced up into the sky and somehow stayed.

"Ah, ya can't beat these taildraggers," Dave yelled over the engine. "Most forgiving beast they ever made." As if to demonstrate his point he took his hands off the controls, and the plane leveled off by itself about five hundred feet up, while Dave rolled the trim wheel a few degrees.

". . . Yeah, I got a '46 wife, a '46 plane, a '46 truck. Musta' been my year."

But my attention was outside, for when the trees fell away, we found ourselves floating over a richly-colored, intricate world of land and sky and water.

"Vinalhaven is a natural place for a spotter plane, but no one was really doing it until I came along," he went on. "They were trying to cover all this in outboards f'chrissake. . . ."

On the western horizon, yellow then with the sun just down, was the blue

"A thick fog is a queer thing, robbing your vision, distorting sounds."

line of the mainland hills, stretching from south to north. Tucked into them here and there, the tiny shapes of buildings, a toy town, a church steeple, jutted above the green carpet of forest.

"I can do in half an hour what would take them all evening to do, and I'll see fish that they might miss. . . ."

I could see why. Below was a maze of islands and rock piles, big ones and little ones, mile after mile of intricate winding waterways, and yet but for a few scattered houses on Vinalhaven, there was hardly the hand of man to be seen. The water, reddish yellow, reflected the sky; the entire mass formed a separate microcosm, an archipelago distinct and apart from the other landmasses around the bay, surrounded by open water on all sides.

And here and there, in little coves, were more dories. It was obvious catching herring was pretty serious business around the island.

"Yeah, you've just about got to have a plane in a place like this—just too much territory to cover in a skiff. . . ." The pilot wiggled his hand on the stick, his feet on the rudder pedals. "C'mon, as long as you're up for the nickel tour, you may as well learn to fly one of these things."

My head still spun from the tequila. I hesitated.

"C'mon, it's easy. . . ."

Gingerly, I grasped the stick before me, did as I was bid, and the plane rolled and nosed up and down with my hands to guide it.

Dave pointed and I went, trying to get the feel for it all, the plane responding easily to my hesitant touch.

Below us the harbor slid by, with Amaretto lying peacefully at the wharf, a postcard scene. And yet on both sides of the harbor mouth was a wild and remote coast with few houses, the trees coming down to a rocky and deeply indented shore.

With each cove, each dory, we floated over, Dave would explain, "Yeah, that's Wharf Cove there, Peter's gang tends that one," or, "We call that one Deep Hole, and it's one of Jim's." Each cove, as in South Bristol, had a dory in it, "belonged" to someone.

Dave took over and we worked east and then north as the light slowly faded from the sky. Over each cove Dave would put the plane into a shallow bank and look out and down into the water. Over one, we went into a steep bank; peering intently down, he let the plane drop to within a few hundred feet of the water before shaking his head and leveling out again.

"Aw, I thought there might be a little bunch in there, but I can't see anything. . . ."

The land got wilder, the shore bolder, with fewer coves. The yellow sky on the horizon gave way to purples and reds, and suddenly we were above the Thorofare, the channel between Vinalhaven and North Haven, the other major island in the Fox Islands. On either side of us lights winked on in large, stately houses with lawns sloping down to the shore, and for a moment we floated above the town of North Haven, a little jewel of a village. A fleet of yachts lay in the Thorofare; there was hardly a workboat to be seen. It was like something out of Fitzgerald, the Twenties, totally different from the world we had just come from.

But as quickly as it had come, it was gone, and then we were above a wild and lonely world of rugged, dark, thickly timbered islands where not a house or a light could be seen.

As the last of the light began to fade from the sky, I remembered uneasily that the landing strip was unlighted, in the middle of a dark wood.

Suddenly we went hard over into a dive. We leveled out just above the trees of a little cove, circling in a hard tight bank, Dave's eyes intent on the water below. Finally he pointed down and yelled back to me.

"There the little bastards are, see 'em?"

I looked along his arm, but saw nothing. The sky was dark, the water featureless.

"Look off that point, look for the bottom. It's sand there—it'll be a little lighter, you'll be able to see a darker patch on top of it. Look close now, they're even moving a little bit."

He pushed the stick forward, the throttle back, and we settled even lower over the water. I stared and stared, and finally saw them: the faintest shadow, like a dark cloud, along the very bottom of the cove, slinking in from the deep, darker water offshore. I could feel the goose bumps again. It was the same feeling I had had that night with Junior in Christmas Cove.

Then at last the throttle was forward and we were climbing out of the dark circle of trees and water, toward the harbor again, the landing strip beyond. Dave slid his side window back and shoved the antenna of the little walkie-talkie out. He spoke rapid-fire to the boys back at the party.

"Yeah, we're headed in now. You guys get another night to kick back, I guess—there's that same little bunch at White Islands, but they're still right there in that hard bottom, and you'll never be able to hold them. . . ."

He snapped the radio off, slid it back under his seat, banked the plane over the harbor, and settled on a compass course for the dark interior of the island.

I leaned forward, touched his shoulder. "Seal Island, where's Seal Island?"

He jerked his head out to the right, down the bay, past the harbor mouth. "That way, down there ten miles. Look hard, you might be able to just see it."

I looked. Beyond the harbor was the blink of the buoys on the outer ledges, but there was little light on the sea at all. Then, just for a moment, I thought I saw something, far out to sea, on the very horizon—just a low ridge, rising from the ocean.

Yet even from that one glimpse I sensed what the men back in Ralph Gray's General Store had talked about: there was about it a sense of mystery that somehow set it apart from the other islands in the bay.

The engine slowed. I looked ahead—we were on the final approach, but I could see nothing but dark woods. Dave dropped the flaps and we ballooned up a bit; then he cut the engine back to an idle. I felt spruce limbs snatching up at us, and suddenly we were down hard, without a bounce, rattling along the grass and gravel. From out of nowhere came the dog, running, barking, trying to keep up.

40

By the time the plane was back in the barn and we were back in the truck, the sudden silence ringing in my ears, it was full dark, the moon not yet up, the stars bright and cold-looking. The strip in the woods behind us was almost invisible.

"That's cutting it close with the light, isn't it?" I asked.

"Naw," came the answer, "I could find that strip in my sleep."

Later, back at the boat, when all was quiet, I carried 'Wals' up the ladder, and we walked. The harbor was still, all the boats pointed west in the lightest air of a breeze. I could see the wink of the lights on the outer buoys; beyond, invisible in the darkness were Seal Island, Wooden Ball Island, the "Rock," all those places I had heard about and could now—just barely—begin to visualize. I was still awed by that short plane trip, that new world, the intricate maze of islands that had been so unexpectedly revealed to me.

The fog was dungeon-thick the next morning. I could tell it without opening my eyes, for not a single lobsterboat started up, and all sounds had a curious, muted quality. I let my head slide back against the pillow, the first good long sleep in a month.

Later, we had a few hours' work finishing up the sock brailer. It was odd, working in that impenetrable fog—our world ended about twenty feet away in any direction. Even the ladder up to the wharf disappeared into the gray murk.

Before midday there was a commotion in the harbor. We could hear excited voices, and half a dozen boats and outboards starting up. Tom appeared out of the fog, towing two dories with an outboard boat. He was an affable, big guy about our own age, and he paused alongside for a moment.

"What's going on?" I asked.

"Big shut-off in Deep Cove. . . . The lightkeepers came over for groceries, said they could hear all sorts of fish flipping. . . ."

"Hey. All right!" I was happy for them, for I had been told there hadn't been a shut-off around the island that year.

"Don't get too excited," Tom said. "We haven't sold them yet. There's a lot of false alarms in this business. I just hope this isn't one of them."

Then he was gone, and we were left to wonder what was happening out there in the fog.

The fog never lifted, but before dark, Jim stopped by in his outboard boat. He seemed excited.

"C'mon along in the morning if you want. . . . We'll load you, all you want. Plenty of market, too."

"You got 'em, then."

He shrugged. "They're behind the twine, but there's a big swell runs in there that lifts the bottom of the net on the high water, so we want to sell 'em as quick as we can."

Next morning, in my naivety, I thought it was this simple: get a load of herring, bring it into the harbor, and the lobstercatchers and dealers would line up to pay cash money for it.

A thick fog is a queer thing, robbing your vision, distorting sounds. And when we were ready to leave, to get our first herring at last, the fog was still incredibly thick. It made me uneasy. We had come in daylight, and had seen the ledges and reefs on all sides of the harbor mouth. Our destination now was a cove around the other side of the island, reached through a narrow channel between rocks and the shore, where there was little room for error.

Carefully as I could, I tuned the radar and made all ready. Then Ann threw the lines off the dock, and the land was no more.

Radar is an imperfect tool—a television-like screen showing a series of blotchy shapes that could be rocks, boats, islands, or buoys. A lobsterboat and a bell buoy might look identical on a radar screen, and a narrow channel can disappear right into the middle of the screen, too close for detection. When that happened, I'd take the boat out of gear and send Ann up to the bow, and she would peer anxiously ahead, smelling the spruce in the woods close on both sides, hearing the splash of the swell on the rocky shore. Then the constriction would be behind us, the channel would open up on the screen, and the radar would show us the way again.

We picked our way uncertainly. Finally we rounded a point and felt the heavy ocean swell lift and drop the boat beneath us. The radar showed a cove with many boats. We anchored in an out-of-the-way corner and settled down to wait.

With engine and radar dead, the sounds suddenly seemed loud and close. There would be the oomph of a sea running up a long beach, a moment of stillness, and then the gravelly rush of water retreating, moving the gravel and stones of the beach with it. There were the sounds of engines and voices, and every ten seconds or so, drowning out everything else, the deep blast of the horn at the lighthouse.

After a few hours the fog lifted a bit, and a wild and lonely spot was revealed—a wide cove backed by steep beach and thick, dark woods, and full that morning of boats and men.

From point to point stretched an unbroken curve of net, the corks clearly visible at the top of each swell, sealing off the cove, trapping the fish. But all activity was at the very center, where a big carrier, twice our size, lay with anchors out fore and aft and men in dories and skiffs working in a shrinking rectangle of net beside her. Four men in yellow oilskins were hand hauling a net from a big dory, pulling in unison, drawing themselves closer and closer to the big carrier. The men aboard the carrier, the skiffs, and the dory looked down into the dark water, waiting.

Ann and I took the outboard boat and went over to watch. It was new to us, and we weren't exactly sure what the men were doing, but the drama was intense, palpable. The men pulled, took up the slack, and pulled again. No one spoke. There was only the gravelly rush of the sea on the shore, and the moan of the foghorn. All engines were silent, all voices stilled. All of us waited, expectant, looking down into the water.

Then a commotion. A few silvery fish swam up out of the depths, and suddenly, with little warning, the entire area between the dory and the carrier was solid, bright, boiling herring, a pool maybe fifteen feet in diameter. The sound they made was like none I had ever heard before: the rushing, flipping sound of a million herring tails all beating the water at once in a mad frenzy to escape.

The men in the dory stopped, leaned back, lit smokes. It was done. On the carrier, an engine started up and the men lowered a thick black hose in among the fish, and in moments a bright stream of herring was shooting down into their hold.

We watched as the carrier sank lower and lower in the water, and inside of a half hour it was done, her holds full with herring spilling onto the deck. A big skiff towed her clear of the net while another carrier jockeyed into position, and the whole business began again. First the outboard boats buzzed back and forth, working from the shore out toward the line of net. Then the men in the dory set their seine in a circle. They pulled on a line through the rings along the bottom of the seine, "pursing" the net and making it into a basket, trapping the fish. Then they hauled in the twine by hand, "drying up" the net, making the basket smaller and smaller until at last the moment came, the water boiled and the fish were on the surface, and the pump started up.

"The men pulled, took up the slack, and pulled again. No one spoke."

Three boats they loaded there, each until it would hold no more. The fog would roll in thick, temporarily hiding all but the shore and the nearest boats. Then another big carrier, high in the water, would appear, maneuvering carefully toward the line of corks. Her crew would drop anchors fore and aft, the pump would start up, and she would sink lower and lower in the water, until finally, fully loaded, she would disappear once again into the gray wall. One set of the net might yield up eighty or a hundred thousand pounds of fish. I was awed at the sheer volume of herring trapped in that little cove.

At last, after so many months of work, we were about to get our first load of fish, to make some cash money.

But then one of the men called over to us.

"You got any market left?"

"Sure, plenty of market." It had been all arranged—the lobster buyers were out of bait, and they'd said they'd take my fish.

"Well . . . that guy's headed into the harbor, and he's sure loaded with something. . . ." The fog had lifted a little, and he nodded his head toward a dirty, rust-streaked sardine carrier, heavily laden and headed around toward the harbor from the west.

"They're in the bait business too, and by the looks of things I'd say he just shot you out of the saddle." Then he was gone.

We got the outboard going and made the harbor just in time to see the boat, the Bay Lady, tie up beside the cinder block bait building of the largest lobster and bait dealer in the harbor. They rigged a huge hose, easily a foot in diameter, up into the building, and began pumping fish into the bait tanks. A few feet shorter than us, but beamier, Bay Lady was poorly kept up, and she gave off that particularly pungent smell I was to learn so well—rotten herring.

"Hey, what the hell's the deal? I'm about to start loading herring out there, and you said you'd buy half a trip." I confronted the man I'd spoken with earlier.

He shrugged, nodding toward a line of lobsterboats below his wharf, waiting for bait. Then he looked at his watch.

"Sure, that was this morning. We waited, but . . ." his voice trailed off.

I went into the storage building where he kept his bait tanks to look at the fish he was getting. The stench almost pushed me right back out the door. The mess coming out of the hose from the Bay Lady was barely recognizable as fish—a red, bloody syrup, with chewed up herring parts in it. The men in the building were shoveling salt onto it as fast as they could, but even I could tell it wouldn't last long in such hot weather.

I called the dealer in.

"You call that stuff bait? It's half rotten before you even get it."

He grimaced, but stayed outside. It was clear he wasn't any too pleased either.

"When you're out, you got to get what you can." He shook his head, then lowered his voice, nodding over at the Bay Lady. "That guy, he pumps his fish too hard. See those?"

The back deck of the Lady was covered with blue plastic bushel baskets filled with what looked like herring scales mixed with blood and intestinal matter. The whole mess was swarming with flies.

"Scales, see, that's where he makes his money. He sells the herring, and then he sells the scales that come off in the pump, makes it twice that way." He lowered his voice a little more. "Nothing wrong with selling scales. Everyone does that, it's part of the business. But that guy's too greedy. He's got a couple of big knotted ropes up inside his pump hose, beats up the fish to get more scales. You don't have to do that. . . ." He shrugged again. "But I've got to have herring, even if it's that shit. . . ."

I went around to the other lobster dealers, but the story was the same—the shrug, and sorry, but the Lady had come in first.

We motored slowly out of the harbor, past the Bay Lady. The smell was nauseating. Her skipper gave us a nice, friendly wave.

"What a jerk," Ann said.

It was as though someone had taken a thousand dollar bill that you *really* needed, snatched it right out of your hand. Only it was worse. We'd spent months making Amaretto something to be proud of, only to be aced out of our market by a boat whose odor made us gag.

We motored back out, hugging the shore, to where Amaretto was anchored. We decided we'd just lie there for a while. There was a jug in a drawer underneath my bunk.

We opened it.

But in two days of sunny weather, with every boat fishing lobsters, the bait supply was depleted, and one of the dealers agreed to try half a load from us. I asked Jim about getting a load of fish from him.

"Plenty of fish," he assured us cheerily. "Chase us to M'hegan, and we'll load you easy."

So off we went, following the Nighthawk out of the harbor and down the bay.

But, oh she was *small*. There was a fair-sized sea on, and seen from astern, it always looked as if the next wave would overwhelm the little forty-footer.

She also had a curious feature from her life as a herring seiner. To keep the boom from swinging, a line from the end of it was always made fast to one of the ring bolts in the stern and hauled tight with the winch. Over the years this had put a twist in her, one side of the stern being noticeably higher than the other.

She was, as they say, pretty much "all used up."

Naturally we had assumed that Jim was going to Monhegan to fish for us. But when we arrived, there was another sardine carrier, the big Jacob Pike, also there for "plenty of fish."

It also developed that the other boat was first in line for "plenty of fish." It seemed that the sardine company that owned the other boat, provided some of the nets and gear that Jim used. They also paid more money for the fish. . . .

We turned off all but our masthead light. It was an unexpected, eerie experience to be lying there, a little way off the island, listening to the rush of the

45

sea against the cliffs and the cries of sea birds swooping down on us from nowhere.

Jim was but the dimmest shape, seen now and again, in and out of the fog. The other carrier shadowed him, the three of us doing a little dance in the night.

And unseen or heard, but still somehow sensed, felt, was a fourth presence: a school of herring. I became aware, as I had before in the cove with Junior that night, of a duel, a contest between the men and the fish. Jim feinted, jockeyed for position, trying to put the boat in just the right spot to get the net around them.

He relied almost totally on a sonar unit. It sent out a beam of sound around the boat, which displayed the fish and the bottom on a TV-like screen beside the radar.

In order for him to make a successful set of his net, he had to position himself downwind of the school, with the fish on his righthand, or starboard, side

"For a long while there was nothing but the black, dripping net sliding up out of the deep."

because the Nighthawk was rigged so that she could only circle to starboard to set the net. Furthermore the fish had to be in a compact enough body so that he could circle them without running out of net, and they had to be in deep enough water so that the net wouldn't hang up on the bottom, most likely ripping.

The night grew late, and the school of fish was in on the rockpiles, Jim said, where to set the net would be to chance losing it.

"We'll wait until they move off into the deep, just before morning. Then we'll have a crack at them."

Hours passed. The fog thinned, grew thick again. I lost track of the boats, the time. Finally I jogged offshore to get clear of the cliffs and fell into the bunk, half asleep.

"Got 'em." The radio spoke: it was Jim. I got up, started the engine, and headed over to the two shapes on my radar, a mile off the cliffs. I approached them gingerly, watching for the net.

Then a glow appeared in the fog ahead, and a strange scene emerged: a circle of light, the two boats at the center of it, rising and falling with the swells. The men peered down into the water between the boats as they worked to bring the net up, and the boats came closer and together, until suddenly the water boiled silver with fish. The hose was lowered and the loading began.

Finally we'd get our fish, I thought, and Ann and I got ready.

But it was just a small set, and the carrier wanted more. They set again and again until the first light began in the east. Each set was smaller than the one before it.

The radio gave us the news:

"Not much of a chance now, with the light coming on, Joe. Why don't you just lie here today, walk around the island, and we'll be along at the edge of dark. . . ."

So discouraged and very tired, we felt our way into that strange harbor and dropped the anchor. It was midmorning before I woke. The fog was still thick around the boat, but I could hear the surge of the sea on the shore close at hand and the barking of a dog.

I smelled fresh coffee from the fo'c's'le, so I went below, sat wearily down. Corn got off Ann's bunk to come over and lean heavily against my leg.

"Plenty of fish," Ann said.

"Plenty of market," I answered bitterly.

"And the worst part is that now I'll have to find a phone and call those guys and tell them we didn't get any fish . . . Aggh!" I was pretty disgusted, tried to put it all from my mind.

But the coffee was good, and she had made fresh rhubarb muffins, and Cornwallis thumped his tail under the table for treats. It took the edge off my discouragement.

After a bit we poked our heads out the hatch to watch the shapes emerge from the fog as it thinned out. First came a lobsterboat, almost touching our stern, for the harbor was narrow, then a little skiff, then the wharf, and finally a three-story hotel, overlooking it all.

47

By and by we went ashore. But where we expected taciturn men and piles of lobster traps, perhaps a net being mended on the wharf, instead we found ladies in curlers walking poodles, men in elegant summer clothes, an artist's colony, and we felt queer and out of place.

At the stone wharf in the harbor a man was loading trash into his lobsterboat, great green garbage bags full of it, covering the entire back deck—all the trash from the town, the three-story hotel, the curio shoppes and snack bars. On the wharf above, a couple watched, the harbor around them a pastel postcard, a study in muted grays and greens. The woman called down to the man in the boat.

"Hello . . . say, where does all that stuff go? I mean, the island's so clean, do you take it over to the mainland for burning?"

The man in the boat, finished with his chore, threw the lines off, sparing a moment for the woman on the wharf. "Naw, I just take it around the point and dump it over the side. The ocean carries it away. . . ."

With the night came the fog. From the windows of the huge hotel over our heads, great shafts of light stabbed out into the swirling gray. Women in dresses, men in sport coats wandered over to the head of the wharf, looked curiously down at us where we lay. With our radar antenna rotating slowly, our engine ticking over, and the steady low chatter of voices on the radio, we must have seemed from a very different world to them, and they stayed, watching in fascination.

"Come in easy now; we got a good set here. Stay clear of those corks," the radio spoke. It was Jim, talking to the Jacob Pike.

I expected it would be another couple of hours to load, get the net straightened around and find another bunch of fish to set on for us, so I half dozed in my bunk.

But then there was a call for us: "Amaretto, come on . . . these're too feedy for the fact'ry. We'll hold 'em for you . . ."

I yelled for Cornwallis who was making friends with the natives ashore. He thumped down aboard; then Ann had the lines off, and the dock and the hotel disappeared into the fog behind us.

"Steer, will you?" Turning the wheel over to Ann, I buried my head in the radar screen. It was too complicated for me to look at the radar and steer at the same time in such a constricted anchorage. Besides, there was nothing to be seen outside but fog. So I called out the directions and Ann steered:

"Ahhhh . . . come right a hair . . . that's good, hold it there. . . ."

I had the radar on the shortest range, the screen only representing the area of a circle a half mile in diameter. But still, the harbor was very narrow and crowded, and I felt as if we were threading a needle as we moved through it and into the open water outside.

The darkness was inky. Amaretto rose and fell in the swell. Finally there was a glow in the fog ahead, and gingerly, with the big air-filled poly "balloons" out as fenders, we slowly slid in alongside the Nighthawk, careful of his net, our propeller.

Tom came aboard for a moment to show us what to do—tie off their corkline, the top of their net, to our rail. Then he was back with the others.

The power block at the end of the boom brought most of the net back aboard, and the men worked below it, arranging the net on the stern of the boat as it descended from the block. Getting the fish up at the very end was the back-breaking part. At the rail of the boat was a "power roller," a rotating length of 6-inch pipe with rubber cleats to help draw the net, heavy laden with fish, out of the water. But the bulk of the work fell on the backs and shoulders of the crew.

For a long while there was nothing but the black, dripping net sliding up out of the deep—that same powerful moment of waiting that had so struck me before. But it went on longer, ten minutes maybe, and no one spoke, and I thought that they had missed the fish.

Then all at once there they were—flipping and boiling, silvery white on the top of the water, making that sound again, the distinct rushing sound of the tails all beating frantically on the surface at once.

"Now there's a good bunch 'fer 'ya." The men leaned back, rested; their part was done.

Now it was time to see if the sock brailer worked.

We swung the boom out over the fish. Ann stood by the winch lever, I by the long handle of the dipnet, and we began. She would lower the winch, while I drove the big hoop into the fish. Then it was up with the winch, and a few hundred pounds of fish would slide up the tube of net into the hold.

But the net proved too long, and the loading was slow and tedious, two hours to load the after hold with 40,000 pounds, where a regular carrier with a fish pump could load that in half an hour. And suddenly those twenty tons seemed like a *lot* of fish. I was worried about selling them, what I would have to do with them if I couldn't. I waved to Jim that I had enough.

"Naw, take 'em all; there's just a little handful left. They're dead now, anyway, may as well take 'em." Jim and the whole gang were emphatic.

The "little handful" was another twenty thousand pounds. It filled both holds of Amaretto up to the very top, "plugged 'er," until there were fish spilling out onto the deck.

We cleaned up the deck, put the hatch covers on, squared away the boom, got the boat shipshape for the run back up the bay for home. Jim quickly disappeared away into the black, and when Ann spoke, her voice had a quaver.

"I guess we're supposed to be this low in the water, huh?"

Our usual five feet of freeboard had shrunk to a foot or less, and in the stern, behind the pilothouse, the water was almost slopping over onto the deck.

Even Cornwallis, thoughtfully chewing a herring, looked uneasily at the water so unexpectedly close.

And the wind had begun to blow.

I tried to be casual.

"Oh, yeah, all these sardine carriers, they really settle when they're loaded."

Believing what I had told her, she and Cornwallis went down into the fo'c's'le after we were all cleaned up and slept easily.

I put the engine in gear, and we began to slide through the water. The night was very black; outside the windows was nothing. Inside there was only the dimmest red glow from the compass and the pale green images on the radar screen.

And in that dark pilothouse, my fears crowded in on me again. I left the wheel a few times, slid around to the back, down into the engine room to check things over. The bilge was dry and everything was as it should be. But coming up the ladder and looking over the stern did little for my confidence. Loaded as we were, the huge propeller pushing our stern down, I could see that our wake, glowing faintly from the phosphorescence in the water, was easily two feet above our deck.

Amaretto was sixty years old. I had bought her without a survey; the condition of the fastenings holding her together was anyone's guess. Our outboard skiff was ashore. By the time we had gotten her all together and ready to go, there hadn't been money for a dinghy or survival suits. If a few fastenings did let go, if a plank popped off, she'd be gone in minutes, and probably us with her, for the Nighthawk was a good way up the bay by then.

Twice, flashlight in hand, I crept up the dark deck, slid the fo'c's'le hatch quietly back, and shined my light down. All was well. Ann and Corn were asleep on the bunk, the faint aroma of dinner still lingering in the warm air. I'd close the hatch, turn, and behind me in the stygian black would be Amaretto's running lights shining out into the fog, hanging suspended in the night.

The worst part was the back channel, in through the rockpiles the first time in night and in fog. I memorized the chart, but then the wind came on, blowing harder and harder. The seas piled up, and on the radar the targets came closer and closer to us. They looked different from what I expected, and I could find no channel.

The foghorn on the point boomed loud and close; we were very near the rocks. My heart beat heavily in my chest.

Then when there was no time or searoom left, a little dark alley opened up on the radar screen between glowing targets on either side, and I took it.

I opened the pilothouse door, saw the glowing backs of breakers a hundred feet to port, smelled the wet pine and spruce close at hand.

Trusting all to shimmering green shapes on a radar tube, we twisted and turned between invisible reefs and islets, and finally where the screen showed boats, the harbor, I slowed and took the engine out of gear.

A dim glow appeared ahead, became a light on the wharf. We were back.

Ann appeared, wearing a parka, rubbing her sleepy eyes.

"Umm," she said. "I slept well."

Once in the harbor, with only the faraway rush of the wind in the trees and the murmur of the surf outside, my fears coming up the bay seemed foolish. I collapsed into the pilothouse bunk, hoping for a bright fair morning, when all the lobster fleet would want to be off, and all would need our bait.

Because our competitor, the scummy Bay Lady, also sold bait in Vinalhaven and had been in business for over a year, we had to have an edge over him somehow, or we'd never get a foothold.

So when I was steaming back up the bay, I hit upon the idea of "Home of the Big Bushel." Bait was sold by the bushel basket, and Carl, captain of the Bay Lady, was well known for giving a short bushel. I intended to jam every herring that would fit into my baskets.

So there we were, with thirty tons of herring, strangers in a strange harbor. Our business consisted of little more than a "fresh bait" sign Ann had painted up the day before. I felt a little like a man with a fiddle or guitar, setting up on the street corner, his hat before him.

A lobster dealer had expressed a desire for a few hundred bushels, but we were loaded with eight hundred. We had to sell all we could to the passing lobsterboats.

The Vinalhaven boats, like most inshore lobsterboats, usually baited up every day, and each needed between five and ten bushels. Sometimes they'd bait up in the evening when they sold their lobsters, but more often in the morning on their way out of the harbor. By giving them fast service and better "measure"—or the "big bushel," as we fancied it—we hoped to get ahead of the Bay Lady and bypass

"So there we were, with thirty tons of herring, strangers in a strange harbor."

51

the lobster dealers who looked upon storing and selling bait as a tedious but necessary part of their business.

But the first engine started up late, and as I rolled over in my bunk, I saw the reason and groaned—fog, thick enough to keep much of the fleet in. Desperately hopeful, I had my jeans on and was out the door in t-shirt and bare feet, getting a tie-up line ready. But the boat turned away, headed out the foggy harbor entrance instead, and my heart sank.

Another one started up, but I simply lay back on the bunk, determined not to be let down again. Then a tired-looking boat idled past, saw the "fresh bait" sign, and swung around curiously. I was on deck in a flash and the pitch began:

"Yep, right over here, pal, Amaretto bait, the freshest in town . . . annnnnd . . . the home of the *BIG* bushel."

Wordless, expressionless, oblivious to my pitch, a large, florid-faced man took my line, wrapped it around the rusty pipe stanchion holding his lobster pot hauler. He had great hams for hands, sticking out of a checked shirt that was festooned with pieces of dried bait.

"Where'd 'ya 'git them herrin'?"

He stepped aboard, picked up a fresh fish off the top of the hold, rubbed it between his fingers, crushed it, smelled it, and wiped the whole bloody mess off on his trousers.

"Monhegan. Last night."

"Huh." He picked up another herring, studied it, dropped it back into the hold. He looked around our boat, slowly, as if he was searching for something he couldn't see.

"Where's 'yer pump?"

"Oh, we brail them; we haven't got a pump." I kicked the brailer lying over by the rail.

He got back aboard his boat and pulled the tops off a couple of old wooden barrels. One got emptied over the side, a nauseous mess of fish guts, eyeballs and maggots.

"Twelve bushels," he said, and our new venture began. I started the engine, called down to Ann in the fo'c's'le, and then we were hustling, she running the winch, me shoving the plastic bushel baskets into the fish, filling them right up to the very top, a good bushel and a quarter at least, and swinging them over to the lobsterboat, keeping up a steady line of bullshit all the while. "Yeah, 'ya can't do any better than *this* bait, nosirree*bob*. Guaranteed to catch lobster you didn't even know were there." He ignored me, taking the baskets as I swung them over, dumping them in the barrels, mixing them with salt.

The best was the end, when he had what he wanted. He plucked a thick wallet from next to the compass, and with a twisted dark thumb and forefinger, looking more like tree roots than anything else, pulled seventy-odd bucks out. Behind him, milling in the harbor in the fog, were a few other boats, curious, waiting.

He waited around for a moment or two, standing there, with his tie-up line in his hand, undecided about something. He looked curiously at the boat again, and finally he spoke:

"She's the old Muriel, ain't she? You kids fixed her up."

I nodded.

"Huh. Thought so." Then he threw off the line and chugged off into the fog.

But for the waiting boats, I would have hugged Ann, danced a little jig, to have made some money at last. For a few hours we were euphoric, loading boats, taking in money.

But the pile of herring in the hold went down ever so slowly, and most of the boats just lay on their moorings.

And on the third morning, when the sun burned through at last, a day "t'haul," as the lobstercatchers would have it, a third of our herring were still aboard, bloody and decaying. The stinking Bay Lady was lying at the head of the harbor with Carl's version of fresh herring, and none would have ours.

So we went outside the harbor, found a spot between the ledges where there was none to witness our shame, and Ann and I alternated the awful job of standing hip-deep in rotten herring, filling the baskets to swing overboard.

"Plenty of fish" she called tauntingly.

"Plenty of market," I called back.

By and by a zippy little lobsterboat stopped alongside and a sharp faced man asked if we would give him some of the bait we were throwing away. So we passed him five bushels, and he dumped a bucket of short lobsters on our deck and was off.

I looked at the little critters for a moment. Rotten herring for illegal lobsters, probably an even trade, I thought. But then what little pride I had left surged up, and I flipped them back over the side.

We were finally in business.

Five

The following evening just at six, when we felt down on our luck and even further down on our money, two large and freshly painted sardine carriers, the Pauline and the Delca, slid into the harbor to lie beside us.

The men from the Pauline came aboard, looked over all that we had done, and expressed, in few words, their pleasure that the old boat was being cared for again. They went on to say that our boat had belonged to the same cannery as theirs and that the boats had worked side by side for decades, that it was good to see them together again.

Their kind words and the presence of those two gleaming and spotless carriers, the flagships of the fleet along this whole coast, made us feel proud again, and we needed it just then.

They invited us aboard, poured a couple of rum and cokes in their deep and cozy fo'c's'le. Above us we could hear pickup trucks pulling up to the wharf and men "hullo"ing down to the boat. In a few minutes the fo'c's'le was full of men, and we all had a few good warm R&C's before the nightly chase after the wily herring began.

The talk was of herring, of Seal Island, all those places I had heard so much about throughout the winter as I had struggled to get Amaretto together.

After a while we finished our drinks and climbed the steep stairs; it was time to go. Outside there was night, cool fog on our faces, engines starting up, radar antennas rotating as the fleet got underway.

And so at last we left for Seal Island—in the fog and in the black, a couple of good, stiff R&C's under our belt, and the fleet around us only radio voices and radar targets.

Of the island that night, we saw nothing. It was lost in the wet, grey murk. We found bottom close to shore on the north side, dropped anchor, and waited.

As soon as the engine was silent, we could hear the cries of birds, swooping all around us, chasing insects, I supposed. It was a strange, soft sound, like a newborn's cry. Petrels, I was told later—storm petrels, nesting only on Seal Island and other remote and little peopled spots.

Far away were faint sounds of engines and voices. But around us was only inky blackness, and the storm petrel's call.

We got our fish early for a change. Jim's herring were too "feedy"—their bellies so full of plankton that they would spoil too rapidly to be canned. After loading us, he would have to try to find a different school of fish, or wait until later in the night. He held the fish alive in the net until we hauled our anchor and found them, a glowing sphere in the black.

Now and then as we loaded, I'd step into the pilothouse for a moment to look into the radar and check our position. The bold south shore of the island was so close that it merged right into the center of the screen, fifty yards away at most. But around us, there was no sign of it, only the peculiar hollow echo of our exhaust off the high cliffs, and the cry of the birds through the fog.

55

An hour's work and we had our trip—the recut brailer worked smoothly. When we were done, both holds neatly topped off (for I had more confidence now about selling), there were some fish still in the net. Jim waved to his men, they let the end of the net back down into the water, and we all watched as the fish swam away groggily, warily, silver under our lights, disappearing into the black water.

Just seventy minutes later, we lay at the wharf in Carver's Harbor again. There were lights in windows, faint music through the fog, the rattle of a pickup truck on a potholed street.

Ann headed down into the fo'c's'le, but I hoisted 'Wals up the ladder to shore, and we walked, the trip to Seal Island still vivid in my mind.

For all that time, from when we left the dock to when we returned again, we had been in thick fog, guided only by pale electronic images. Yet still, though I had not even really seen the island up close, Seal Island again made a powerful impression on me.

For Vinalhaven, though fifteen miles offshore, surrounded by the sea, was still, for all that, a place of the *land*. There were houses, gardens, phone poles, kids on bikes.

Who would have thought that so close, little more than an hour beyond the mouth of the harbor, would be a place so wild, so different, a place so much of the *sea*?

It would be two more trips to the island before I would really see it at all. Even now, when I know the island so well, the image of that first night down there still hangs in my mind as the truest one—black, foggy, a wild dark place of the sea, not of man or of the land at all.

In the morning our last customer was a quiet-spoken older man in a tidy outboard boat, a wooden high-bowed skiff known locally as a Novi. He seemed not to be in a hurry.

"How come you're not charging out at five like the rest?" I asked.

"Well, when you're on social security, you can't be too fierce about it all," he shrugged. "I have my 125 pots, and when it's a good chance, I'll go."

"Did you ever go to Seal Island much?"

The man looked around to see if any other boats were waiting. No one else was moving in the harbor; everybody who was going to haul had already left. He began stuffing the herring into little grapefruit-sized knitted bait bags, tying each one neatly and tossing it into another plastic basket.

"I used to have a powerboat," he began. A powerboat is an inboard lobsterboat with a cabin. "I fished around Seal Island. Everyone did. Sometimes we'd camp there, try to shut off herrin'."

His tanned face seemed to shine a little bit with the memory.

"Those were good days, the camping and the waiting. . . ."

He filled a few more bait bags, looking out at the punts lying on the moorings in the harbor. A light sou'west breeze came and rippled the surface, and all the little boats swung into it.

"When I was a boy, my father told me once that in a bad winter storm, the kind that takes the wharves and fish houses with it, at Seal Island sometimes a huge sea would break right over the island."

PAULINE BATH ME

He hesitated for a moment, as if he weren't sure of the truth of what he was going to say next.

"He said that when that happened, the sea was claiming Seal Island again as its own. . . ."

He stopped again to watch a high-nosed fifty-footer come into the harbor, one of the lobster smacks, boats that transported lobsters over to the mainland. It slowed and tied up at the buyer's station on a little float across from where the ferry landed.

"I must have believed him, I guess. Each time we had a wicked gale, I'd be at the window with the binoculars. . . ."

"Ever see anything?"

"Why yes," he said. "But I got discouraged at first, looking down the bay each time we had a winter blow. I'd about given up on it, thought that it wasn't true. Then when I was fourteen we had a terrible blow, the worst I'd ever seen then . . . all afternoon the wind shook the house and I waited. There was an awful sea on, and I thought it might be the day after all. . . ."

"Was it?"

Jacob Pike and Amaretto at Seal Island: "Who would have thought that so close, little more than an hour beyond the mouth of the harbor, would be a place so wild, so different, a place so much of the sea?"

58

He smiled, "You know how kids are . . . I took the binoculars and went up to the very top of the hill"— he nodded his head toward the hill overlooking the harbor—"up by the water tower, and I looked and I looked, and I could see the spray flying up into the air after hitting those cliffs. . . .

"Finally, when the cold was almost too much, when I was about to give it up and go in, just on the very top of the tide between snow and squalls, I saw it.

"The whole island blurred for a moment, just like it was covered by a white cloud. But I was sure it had been water. I waited and waited for another, until I was about froze, but there was only the one, on the very top of the tide. . . ."

It was a powerful spell the story cast. I suddenly looked around again, remembering where we were, what we were doing.

"Did it ever happen again?"

He shrugged. "Could be, I guess. . . ." Then he went on with his story. "That next summer when we were lobstering there, I went ashore. I had to beg my dad to let me . . . he wasn't a man to stop hauling for some foolishness . . . but finally he put me ashore, and on the very top of the island the big driftwood logs were all moved around, rearranged by the sea. . . ."

A truck stopped above us, and a voice called down, wanting to know if we had any bait left.

The tale of Seal Island was over. The man started up his outboard. "We'll see ya," he said, and moved away.

It was at last light, a few days later, that I first really saw Seal Island. The night was nasty: windy, a sea running, the light dying. I was surprised anyone had gone out; I had secretly hoped they would stay in and we could too. The bait business had revealed itself as an around-the-clock hustle; a night off because of weather would have been a relief.

But at the edge of night we all sailed out of the harbor, steamed for an hour, 189 degrees on Amaretto's old compass.

And then we came upon the island. It was narrow and low, a mile long by perhaps two hundred yards wide. On its north side were two wide bights in a sloping rocky shore; on its south were steep and bold cliffs. Seen from the sea, except for the steep cliffs, it looked an undistinguished sort of place. Yet still, as we came upon it in a windy and forbidding dusk, there was about the island a sense—an aura, almost—of mystery.

Then the night came down all around us, and the island was lost in it. We steamed off to the south'ard, jogging into the wind and the seas. But it was rough, so we let the tide carry us off to the west'ard, around the corner and into a little lee, and there we waited until Jim was ready to set. Then Ann called me out onto the deck and we saw something such as we had never seen before.

Beneath us in the black water huge dim shapes swept by, seemingly the size of locomotives, glowing eerily in the inky darkness. For a moment we were uneasy, until one of them came up to breathe off our stern, and we saw them for what they were—humpback whales—making the phosphorescence of the water fire with their passing.

It was a stunning show. We had it all to ourselves, while the wind made up

59

over our heads, and in the seas around the point the boats were looking for fish and seeing if they wanted to try a set.

On that trip we got a little handful from Jim, and then he and all the others gave it up as too rough. It was on that trip, too, that we met David for the first time.

And when I got to know Seal Island better, it was always David I associated with it. Sometimes I felt that he spent half his life around there, lobstering and catching herring. He fished other places too, but he seemed to be most at ease there, catching them where no one else could. His skill at it seemed uncanny, effortless.

A phone booth, overlooking the harbor and the bay beyond, became my office, and late each afternoon, I'd take a pocketful of coins and start calling around Penobscot Bay, anywhere there was a lobster dealer within six hours' steaming, trying to persuade one of them to take a load of herring from us.

Then, with an idea of what I could sell, I'd call one of the three or four herring seiners around the island to see who could fish for us that night. Ideally we tried to go with someone who didn't have any other market that night so we could be "first boat."

"Plenty of fish, plenty of market," disguised a business that was as cutthroat as any I had ever been in. Not only did we have to struggle to sell our fish, we had to struggle to get them.

Behind the scenes, always working against us, was our competitor, Bay Lady Carl. In the beginning I thought it was just a friendly rivalry we had going. I was wrong, as I was soon to learn.

One foggy evening we were about three miles south of Seal Island, looking for the "Gloucester Boys."

"Yeah, and they'll have the 'net that pooched the North Sea,'" one of Jim's gang told us bitterly. He and the others had spent the night in open skiffs, watching a school of herring, waiting for the fish to swim the last quarter mile into a cove where they could be shut off. It had been an all-night vigil for nothing; at first light the fish had moved off into the deeper water instead.

He explained how the giant nets, two hundred and fifty feet deep by a quarter of a mile long, many times the size of local nets, could catch half a million pounds at a whack.

For generations, he told me, boats of all countries had fished herring in the North Sea in Europe. Then the huge seines were developed, and a few boats began working the grounds with them. Within a few years the vast shoals of fish were gone, the smaller boats out of business, whole towns forced to look for other livelihoods.

Indeed, that evening we found large targets on the radar, bigger than any I had seen out there before. It was the "Gloucester Boys."

Carefully, we approached one of the targets, Ann positioned up on the bow, looking for nets. Suddenly a boat loomed out of the fog ahead—lit up like a city with its brilliant lights, a wall of rusty steel, a giant of a seiner. Nearby was a huge skiff holding up the other side of the seine as the boat loaded itself with its fish pump. The skiff alone was as big as some lobsterboats.

We slid past the stern, read the name, called him on the radio, and asked him if he wanted to sell a trip of bait. He was almost full by the look if it, and there were plenty of fish still in his net.

"Ve ain't selling nao fewking bait!" came the blunt response.

We circled again, watching. They finished up, loading the superseiner deep with fish. There must have been fish still in the net, but dead, for we could see the strain on the corkline as the men let it back into the water. Probably enough fish to fill us and more sank away into the depths, wasted.

We tried others, moving in and out of the circle of lights and high technology boats, as they worked what must have been a giant school of fish. Some refused to sell us bait, others refused to talk to us at all, and I felt angry, resentful, territorial—those were *our* fish, dammit, and here were interlopers scooping them all up and refusing to sell even a handful for bait, though the fish were already dead.

And I thought of what I had heard in the coffee shop that morning and of the men waiting in the skiffs, dependent on the same fish that these boats so carelessly dumped, wasted.

At 4 a.m. we gave it up, reluctantly pointing the bow north through the fog. I dreaded the morning—there was a good weather report, the fog would burn off, there would be lobstercatchers and dealers looking for bait, and the Bay Lady was full. We had heard him on the radio, a few hours away to the east, getting a load.

Then the radio spoke:

"Amaretto, we got a bunch left over here, if you want a trip. . . ."

A voice I didn't recognize gave us directions, and we steamed twenty minutes to the northeast, until another boat emerged from the fog, all lit up, pumping fish out of a net. I recognized it—one of the biggest Maine boats, from Deer Isle, east of Vinalhaven.

A big, talkative man took our lines, called out instructions to his crew, and in moments a thick hose was rigged and spilling a bright stream of fish into our hold. All we had to do was to throw a little salt on the fish every now and then— our easiest load yet.

The skipper peered down at us from the bulwarks. They towered over us; Amaretto must have looked tiny and ancient to him.

"My gang loses a steak dinner on account of this, you know. . . ."

I looked up, not getting it.

"That guy on the Bay Lady," he went on, "he promised he'd buy us all a steak dinner once a week, if we didn't sell you any fish. . . ." He laughed.

"Oh, he had 'em all, all those little islands right over a barrel. It was a regular gold mine for him until you boys came along. . . ."

Our radios crackled with a call for him. He went in to answer it; it was the Bay Lady. I could hear the whole conversation.

"Yeah, what 'ya doing, loading that 'brand X' boat there, Walter? I thought we had an arrangement. . . ." Carl's voice was joking, but I sensed a hard edge to it.

"Ah, we just had a little handful left, Carl, we would 'a had to dump 'em if

61

these guys weren't around . . . they were wandering all around and no one would give them a fish . . . 'Sides, a little *competition* never hurt. . . ."

He came back on deck. "I like those lobstercatchers over on Vinalhaven . . . I just couldn't see condemning them to that shit he calls bait."

On deck the pump finally stopped. We had maybe 40,000 pounds, enough for our markets the next day, enough to shoot the Bay Lady out of the saddle in Carver's Harbor, for if we had bait, most of the boats would buy from us.

"Oh, the *money* that s.o.b. made . . . but you get a big set like this, and you take all you want and sometimes the rest of the fish are dead, even when you try to keep them alive . . . so what can you do? It's better to sell 'em to him than throw them away, even if you only get paid for half. . . ."

His crew was hauling the rest of the net aboard, throwing the lines off; the boat was sliding away from us. I realized I hadn't even offered to pay for the fish.

"Hey," I called over to the skipper, "you want some *money* for these fish?"

"Sell 'em first," he yelled back. "And watch out for Carl; he'd do anything to put you out of business. . . ." Then they were gone.

Carl had a few other tricks. Two nights later we worked with a small seiner, a lobsterboat rigged out with a net on her stern for double-duty when the day's lobstering was done. We were up in the Thorofare, waiting for the plane. When Dave finished his nightly check of the coves around the island, we hoped he would have time to spend a few moments looking around for fish. The lobsterboat-seiner lacked the elaborate sonar that enabled most seiners to find fish, so if the plane could help him set the net around a little school, it would save us a long night of looking for the fish with our primitive electronics.

But when finally Dave buzzed us in a long shallow dive and climbed out over the water, it was getting dark and we didn't know if he'd still be able to see. Then after a brief search he appeared to be circling something over by the North Haven shore, but our radios chose that moment to go on the fritz. Each time the plane tried to call us, I'd hear, "Amaretto . . . ," and then the transmission would be cut off. Finally the plane dove on us, and Dave yelled something out the window that sounded like " . . . that ------ Carl . . . " and then he was gone, scooting over the trees to the landing strip in the dark woods.

So for half the night we both searched for fish. At three they set, ripped their net on a sharp pinnacle, and lost the fish. We went alongside each other for a bit, and they pulled their net out on our deck, mending it in the glare of our deck lights. The skipper was a swarthy man with few words; he had been in the herring game since he was a kid. He came over to me when they were done with the net.

"You know who that was don't you?"

"What d'ya mean?" I asked.

"There's nothing wrong with our radios. That was Carl 'buttoning' us."

"Huh?" I still didn't get it.

"Think about it. Every time the plane tried to call us, Carl just hit the mike button on his radio. That'd blank out the call. . . ."

"How do you know?"

He shrugged. "I saw him coming around the corner into the harbor just as we were leaving. He's already got a load on; he sure as hell doesn't want you to get any. . . ."

"Well, that screws you, too. . . ."

"Ah . . . that's the bait biz . . . you bait dealers'd cheat your own mother to make a sale. . . ."

But the next time Carl tried to slip it to us I was ready.

It was a couple of nights later and we were down the bay somewhere, waiting to get a load of fish.

The radio spoke. It was Carl.

"Yeah . . . how's it going for you tonight, Joe?"

Though we were both out to put the other out of business, on the street or on the radio, it was all smiles.

I looked around, made him out a few miles to the northeast, all lit up, loading fish from someone.

"Oh, not too bad, Carl . . . we'll get a trip by and by, I guess. How you makin' out?"

"Yeah, we lucked out tonight. Tommy had a bunch of feedy ones the fac'try didn't want, so maybe we'll have an early one for a change. Where you headed anyways when you get your trip?"

"Matinicus, I guess. . . ." I lied, not about to reveal my plans, because Carl knew that he could only sell bait in Vinalhaven if we weren't around. "How 'bout you?"

" . . . Ah . . . , " a casual yawn, "we're about done here now. We'll just jog on over to Swan's Island with these."

I knew he was lying; I had just sold a trip of bait to Swan's Island, and a fisherman there told me they'd never buy from Carl again. They wanted herring, he had said, not eyeball soup.

"Yeah, well, have a good trip, Carl, we'll see you by and by. . . ."

After a while, someone called us over to load, but I kept half an eye on Carl's lights, after all the tricks he'd pulled. When he was loaded and his deck lights went out, only his running lights could be seen, fading away slowly to the northeast.

When we were all loaded and cleaned up, I went out on the back deck and gave the horizon a good glassing with the binoculars, especially in around the islands, for I thought his running lights had disappeared rather sooner than I would have expected them to.

And sure enough, there hard in along the shore of Isle Au Haut was the dim silhouette of the Bay Lady, lying with no lights, waiting for us to make our move.

So we swung off to the sou'west, toward Matinicus as I had said, and I left our deck lights on a good while so there could be no mistaking our intentions.

I watched the radar closely and soon noticed a target separating itself from Isle Au Haut, running with no lights, heading back toward Vinalhaven. It was Carl, I was sure of it, figuring that without us, he'd have the market all to himself in the morning.

When it looked as if he were pretty well in toward the harbor, I cut our throttle back to half, killed our own lights, and turned north for Vinalhaven.

The noise from our straight stack was a dead giveaway, so when we were still a mile out, I cut her back to an idle and came into the harbor dead slow. We tied up at our usual berth, Ann put up the "fresh bait" sign, and we both hit the sack.

And when the dawn came and we were hustling to sell all we could, when the fleet was all lined up for our bait, and not a single boat for his, I could see him standing on his stern glaring at us. For by then he couldn't go to Matinicus either; it was a high tide show in the inner harbor, and by the time the tide was high enough we'd be there. So it was he that ended up in my little phone booth office, calling all around the bay to find a market for his fish.

With each load of bait sold, we'd have more confidence, be a little more at ease about it all. We were beginning to feel that maybe, after all, we'd at least be able to pay off our debts.

Carver's Harbor was one of the largest lobster ports in Maine, and slowly its fishermen accepted us. They seemed glad to have a sardine carrier working out of their harbor, especially one that they knew so well anyway.

Going out night after night in thick fog honed my senses to a new degree; I could pick up the slightest indication of anything amiss—sometimes better than my radar.

Often, I'd sleep on the way down the bay at night, turn the steering over to Ann and catch a little rest so I could be alert if we ended up steaming all night. But it was habit for me to get up every half hour or so and simply check the radar. When I did this one foggy evening, halfway down to Seal Island, I thought I saw the faintest return, or target, ahead of us, but just once. I figured it was a big offshore lobster buoy; sometimes they show up like that on radar when there's a swell going.

I lay back down, but couldn't sleep. Something bugged me about that radar target. So I got up again and peered down into the radar screen, but there was no sign of what I had seen before. I would have dismissed it, gone back to sleep, but instead, I pulled the throttle back to an idle, took the engine out of gear, and walked up to the bow in the foggy dark to look and listen.

But there was nothing—just the sigh of our bow slicing through the water as we coasted to a stop. I turned around and headed back to the pilothouse.

A sound came out of the night, and it made the skin crawl on my back.

It was the sound of voices, calmly talking, and very close.

I went back up to the bow again and looked out. Amaretto slowly ghosted through the night, and then ahead, I saw a faint light. At first I thought it was a masthead light a good ways away. But then I saw it for what it was, and my heart about stopped: the dimmest light a flashlight with played-out batteries could make, sweeping over a sail. Beneath it in orange life jackets were more than a dozen figures, sitting and standing in a longboat—one of the boats from a survival training school on a nearby island.

My anger got the best of me:

"You ----ing ---holes, out here with no ----ing lights and no ----ing radar reflector, and it would have been my ass if I'd run you over. . . ."

They looked up, startled, at the screaming apparition that had emerged from the fog.

I got control of myself, went back into the pilothouse, and dug around until I found a flashlight, one of those red, floating, $9.95 jobbers with the big six-volt batteries and the curlicue springs on top. They usually lasted about a week with us—then I'd fly into a rage and smash it to pieces when it didn't work any more. They weren't very good flashlights, but this one still worked.

"Here," I said, reversing gently a few feet away and tossing the light over to them, "take this. It's not much, but it's a damn sight better than what you've got. . . ."

Then I put Amaretto in gear again, and we sailed off into the black.

One night early in our baiting career we steamed for hours in the foggy black, close past Seal Island, No Man's Land, Wooden Ball Island—all uninhabited, unlit, never seen, but smelled, felt, sensed. Five times Jim called us, and five times I slowed Amaretto, watched Jim's boat appear slowly out of the black, and slid alongside to take another little handful of fish out of his net.

But fishing was poor, and after the last set, the hour before dawn, Jim came over and stood for a moment on our deck, looking at the meager pile of herring in our hold.

"Can't seem to do too much tonight," he said. "Fish aren't bunching up like they should." He looked weary and discouraged, as did Tom and the rest of his gang, standing on the stern, pulling in the last of the net, in preparation for yet another set. Purse seining set after set for little handfuls of fish was exhausting work.

So we gave it up, and he was gone in the fog and we were alone in the blackness a little to the west of No Man's Land, rolling slowly in the long swell. Ann and I wordlessly cleaned up the deck and got ready for the steam up the bay, and then in through the reefs to the harbor, in thick fog.

When we were finally underway, she steered and I stood next to her, drinking a cup of coffee and peering down into the radar.

"Still think it's morally and aesthetically bankrupt?" Ann said, mimicking the term I had used for the bait business that day we had shoveled our fish into the ocean.

I laughed. It was pretty pleasant in the pilothouse just then—the hum of the engine, the feel of the boat rising and falling in the swell, a little music on the radio.

She was tired and I was too, but we liked to stand a bit those nights, there in the blacked-out pilothouse, steaming up the bay in the fog.

"Ah, a guy could do worse, I suppose. . . ."

Without really articulating it to each other, we had both come to feel that there was an unexpected and powerfully compelling aspect to this business.

Baiting was a hard and a cutthroat racket. When we got fish we got in late and got up early. If we didn't get fish, we were usually out all night anyway. And some days when the market was strong, we'd be selling fish all day and loading fish all night with little rest in between. My back and shoulders ached day and night; sometimes getting out of the bunk after an all-night steam and two hours' sleep was pure agony.

When I walked to the phone booth to make my calls, there were times when I wanted to stay in, rest up. But then I thought of what we owed, what we needed, and how short the season was, and we went out.

And about every time I'd think I had the market sewed up enough so I could relax a bit, the Bay Lady would slip in out of nowhere and stick it to us.

But when we threw the lines off in the evening and headed down the bay or wherever we were bound that night, we'd always feel a tingle of anticipation for whatever the evening would bring, and in a way, it made all the rest worth it. It began to seem as if our lives consisted of two parts. There were summer days, hustling bait around the islands, enjoying a swim or a walk whenever we could, once or twice a week maybe. And then there were nights—pulling on our flannel shirts and heading down the bay in the black. Every night was different, and more often than not would bring some powerful or dramatic new experience, to be savored, remembered, yarned over later.

Amaretto was part of the adventure—a big part of it. Coming alongside a seiner with a netful of fish on a windy and black night, offshore somewhere with no lee, was a tricky business—it had to be done just right; the risk of damage, injury, hitting the net, losing the fish was always there.

And sometimes when we were steaming inbound with a heavy load, I'd pause in my regular engine room tour, listening for a moment to that 30-year-old engine pushing that 60-year-old boat. Amaretto was all I had hoped she would be and more. And sometimes, down there in the middle of all that wood and machinery, now and again for the fleetingest moment, I sensed a determination as great as my own.

Six

Evening, the harbor: Ann and I waited. The Nighthawk, two dories, and an outboard all lay beside Amaretto. Jim, Tom, and the others were stretched out on top of the net enjoying the evening. The low sun was still warm; someone popped a beer and hunkered down to get more comfortable on the twine.

In Jim's hand, the pocket radio spoke:

"Ah, there's a little bunch right here at Wharf Cove . . . but you guys better hang tough right there. Maybe I'll find something that looks a little better. . . ."

The plane disappeared out of sight, but the running commentary continued over the radio:

"Yeah, there's another little bunch outside of Barton's, but they're in that same little hole they were in last night and not moving. . . ."

It was peaceful just then, the harbor full, all the lobsterboats in.

"Sometimes he'll find a bunch right off in a cove, and we'll get 'em easy," Alton, one of Jim's gang, told us.

"Yeah, and other nights he'll think he sees something, and we'll spend all night in the skiffs looking. . . ." One of the others spat and shook his head.

"I'd like to have a nickel for every bushel we shut off last year," said Tom. "You're lucky to keep one bushel in ten that you shut off."

"How come?" I asked. Ten percent didn't seem much of an average.

"Hard bottom, too much tide," he shrugged, "old gear ripping up, not getting set just right, a breeze of wind coming up just when you don't want it . . . a lot can happen and the result's the same—you lose the fish."

The radio again: "Ahhhhh . . . I'm over the Thorofare now. . . . Pretty slim pickings here . . . I'll just keep working my way around to the east side."

"Those fish backed around the corner into Tomb's Cove yet, Dave? That's an awful good berth there." It was Jim on the radio. He was the master of this shut-off business, I had been told; he knew each cove, every acre of bottom.

"Yeah . . . no . . . don't I wish. . . . Nah, there's nothing within a mile of that place. . . ."

This was the nightly ritual with Jim; he'd only go out with the Nighthawk to fish for us if the plane reported no fish near the coves.

The plan suddenly appeared over the trees and circled right over our heads, right over the harbor in a tight bank. We could look up and see Dave looking down.

"Well, what 'cha think, Dave?" Jim picked up the walkie-talkie and called up to the plane. "These fish gonna' come ashore tonight, or should we go and get a trip o' bait?"

Jim made it sound like fishing for us was about as much fun as a good case of the runs.

"Hell," Dave's tinny radio voice cried. "Make your end off right there, and shut off the goddamn harbor!"

For a moment, no one understood. Then all around us, around the whole rocky basin that was the harbor, came a rustling, a stirring in the water, and then fish began flipping and finning. A big school had moved in right under our noses!

Everyone jumped at once. They started up the motor, made the end of the net fast to an iron chain on the wharf, put the outboard in gear and towed the dory across the mouth of the harbor, the net spilling out behind, sealing it off.

There was half a night's work still ahead: laying out the anchors to hold the net against the tide, setting the "pocket" for the fish to run into. When they were done, it would be too late for them to fish for us.

Darkness: the plane had long since landed. The harbor was filled with voices, flashlights, the glow of cigarette butts moving in the night. Ann slept. I hoisted Cornwallis up onto the dock, and we walked the still streets of town, away from the harbor, back into the woods.

When we returned, the harbor was quiet. For a moment before turning in, I stood on deck and looked out, but all was darkness. There was nothing to hint at the school of fish beneath the moored boats, swimming around, seeking a way out, finding none.

In the morning, at very first light, a big company carrier, the Delca, eased into the harbor and lay beside the corks of the pocket where the men were waiting to

"That evening we steamed among the islands and rockpiles of Vinalhaven's west side."

load her. In a short time, it seemed, she was gone. Tom came over to sit with us after the carrier left and all the twine had been piled back into the dories, and I asked him about it. He was about our age, and the three of us were becoming friends.

"Just one load?" I asked. It seemed like a lot of work for what they got out of it.

"Shutting off a hundred hogsheads or a thousand, it's all about the same amount of work."

A hogshead was seventeen and a half bushels; it was the unit of measure in the herring business. Amaretto was a "fifty hogshead boat"; in each hold was a board marked in hogsheads, so that anyone who sold Amaretto fish could step aboard and look down to see how much she was carrying.

"The only way you can make any money on these shut-offs is to get a big bunch and load boats steady for a few days. But, then again, you don't really know what you have until you shut 'em off, either. . . . But these little one-load shut-offs," he shook his head, "it's hardly worth it. . . ."

That evening we steamed among the islands and rockpiles of Vinalhaven's west side. We were tuned to herring radio:

". . . That same bunch off of Deep Cove, might check on 'em after dark if I can't find anything a little more promising. . . ." The plane circled to the south of us, making lazy circles over the coves. "Old Harbor, nothing . . . Peasley's Cove . . . zilch. . . . Ahhhh, it's pretty bleak here. I'm going to take a pass out over White Islands; haven't been out there in a couple of nights. . . ." He swung to the west, crossed over our heads, passed over an island-flecked sound, became just a dot in the sky.

"HOLY SHIT! Jim, get some twine over here as fast as you can hustle it. There's a shitload of fish here, right off White Island Harbor."

Dave's voice was very excited. We looked to the west. The dot in the sky spiraled lower to the islands.

"Nothing anywhere else, Dave?" Jim's voice seemed cool for some reason. "That's quite a hard berth. . . . We've never had much luck there."

"Fer chrissake, there's maybe fifty grand of fish swimming around in there. Maybe you'll get 'em, and maybe you won't, but you gotta try."

Silence. Then a few minutes later from the harbor behind us came two outboards, each towing a dory full of twine, headed toward White Islands.

Sunset: Dave circled over the islands, guiding the men in the dories while keeping an eye on the fish. Finally he swung over to the north, where we were, to find fish for us.

The day died quickly; the plane had time for but one pass. He spotted a small school off the village of North Haven, then he was gone, racing dim purple dusk to his landing strip in the dark woods.

The night grew very black. The sky skinned over; the moon, the stars were gone. It was a dance we did, following Tommy, our seiner for the evening, in and out of the reefs, among the pinnacle rocks beneath the placid dark waters.

Tommy was a "native son." Born on the island, he had fished all his life there, needed no chart, barely even looked at his radar, yet unerringly wove among the rockpiles for hour after hour.

But for us, it was a very different story. We drew fully six feet of water, and the rocks and ledges were many. Time after time we went into places that were marked on the chart by X's, solid reefs. I danced constantly back and forth between compass, sounder, chart, and radar, yet still expected at any moment to feel our oak keel grate on the stony bottom.

He followed the fish along the shore, among moored sailboats, biding his time, giving the fish room, waiting to surprise them in the open water.

We motored along out in the channel. On the bluffs above us were large summer homes, built in an era of few cars and the overnight steamer from Boston. In the windows were people in dresses and sport coats. They held glasses and talked cheerily while a few hundred yards away we stalked the fish in the black.

Below us, around us, the fish clung to the bottom, hugging the rocks, wary of the circling engines.

Tommy dueled the fish. Hours passed. Deep in the night, when the lights in the houses had all gone out, he made his move, scraping just enough off the top of a school of fish to satisfy our markets for the next day.

In the coffee shop the next morning we met tired faces, red and swollen hands. The White Islands shut-off hadn't worked out. The bottom was too rough; the net had ripped again and again.

"You can't set in there; we told him that a dozen times," Tom said disgustedly.

Alton spoke. "That pilot, he sees a few fish and gets dollar signs for eyes. He ought to spend a night out there with us, trying to get the twine back, see what it really means when he's yelling for us to shut off some cove because he sees a few hundred bushels of fish. . . ."

"Sure . . . 'try it', he says. Then he's gone home, sitting around listening to the stereo, having a drink or two. He gets paid off the top so he doesn't care how much twine we pooch in the process. . . ."

"Breakfast and Antiques," said the sign outside the coffee shop. The shop perched on pilings; beneath it the water from the harbor rushed into the shallow pond beyond. The "antiques" were a few rusty tools and old mason jars sitting on a table in the rear. The breakfast was better—bacon, eggs, French toast, hot cakes, coffee.

By noon Amaretto was unloaded and scrubbed down. We packed lunches and walked a few miles to a quarry hidden in the trees. We dove deep into the water from the granite cliffs, swam, and spent the afternoon lying on the rocks, soaking up the warmth, forgetting about the night-and-day struggle we were in.

When we walked down the hill to the harbor, the fog was pouring in from the ocean, thick, like a river around the point. It brought in with it the beautiful Pauline and her sistership, Jacob Pike. They lay beside us; we went below, drank Coke and Bacardi Light, learned of fish to the east and west. Finally it was time to follow them out into the foggy black for another tedious night of "inside" fishing between the reefs and the rocks.

But instead, after running for just half an hour, we found ourselves tying up beside them at the stone wharf on Dogfish Island. We walked up to a lodge of

*"The fog was pouring in from the ocean, thick, like a river around the point. It
brought with it the beautiful Pauline and her sistership, the Jacob Pike."*

72

great chinked logs with a cedar-shingled roof. Outside, the fog was thick and damp; inside, there was a fire in a stone fireplace and a VHF radio on the mantle.

A lanky, sandy-haired woman welcomed us. There were drinks all around, and we sank into the chairs talking. But whenever the radio spoke in its tinny voice, all would stop to listen.

The woman was a friend of the carrier skippers. When the fish were close like this and it was convenient, the boats would lie here at her wharf, engines still running, radars turning, ready to leave on a moment's notice; meanwhile the men would catch a brief visit.

I stepped outside for a moment. The fog had entirely wrapped the house and wharf; of the boats, there were only masthead lights, dimly seen in the black.

The fish were deep, the voices on the radio said—uncooperative, frightened, staying in the deep water or on the hard bottom. Jim was out there, and Tommy in his little boat; the two of them talked back and forth as they looked. David was out there too, somewhere, but from him there was only silence.

The voices on the radio seemed far away, disembodied. The fire crackled in the fireplace, and a little wind began to make up; we could hear the trees start to rustle outside.

It was like a scene from the Thirties or Forties. We could have been sitting around the radio on a farm, lost somewhere in the vastness of the western plains. We could have been listening to an adventure serial, all of us glued to the speaker, our only link to the world beyond the dusty fields and lines of parched trees.

But the drama was real, the players just a mile away, working in the fog, invisible to each other. As we listened, Tommy tore up on the bottom, gave it up, and headed for the harbor.

"Jacob Pike, come on. . . . We got a little handful here. May as well come and get 'em. . . ." It was Jim. His voice sounded discouraged.

An engine started up, and we looked out as running lights moved away from the wharf and were lost in the black.

We stayed on and listened, Ann and I and the Pauline's men. Cornwallis lay in front of the fire, turning over now and again to get even heat.

It was discouraging for Jim—he was getting only a few hundred bushels each time, setting on schools too deep for his net to be really effective, barely scraping the tops off. His usually upbeat voice got more and more tired as we listened.

The fire died away to coals, and the damp cold of the foggy night crept in around the corners of the room. We threw on more logs and watched them blaze up, reflecting on the varnished walls, warming our faces. From David, there was still only silence.

Jim's net, too, finally touched the bottom and ripped up. A "parking lot job," he said, too big a tear to mend on the boat. So he gave it up too, and headed back through the islands and ledges to Carver's Harbor.

A long while passed. We had another round of drinks. It grew late.

73

Conversation faltered, but it was good to listen to the breeze in the trees outside, the stir of the sea on the shore, a log falling in the grate.

Finally the radio spoke, this time a faraway, sleepy voice. It was David:

"Where . . . is . . . the . . . Pauline?"

"Right here." Henry picked up the mike on the mantle.

"Ah . . .," a yawn, "well . . . I got what you want. . . ."

"Goood. . . ." We all got up. "Where are you?"

"Ah . . .," a yawn again, "I dunno . . . lemme look . . .," a long pause. "By the rock, Henry, 'bout a half mile off. . . ."

"Okaaaaay. . . ."

We said our goodbyes, and in minutes we were in the boat. The house and wharf disappeared into the featureless black astern.

Pauline went ahead and we waited a bit, then approached a radar target that became a circle of light. Gingerly we slid alongside the Pauline, on the other side from David's net.

We went aboard to watch. Between the boats was the net, in a pool of black water. David and his three men, all shoulders and arms, were working to bring it up, staring down at the water, straining with the effort of the hard, punishing work. No one said anything.

Time passed and still no one spoke. All peered down intensely into the net. But there was nothing, no movement, no sign of fish. All around us was black, silent, thick fog, the scene around the net a powerful, mysterious tableau.

Then from deep in the water came the glitter of fish, and suddenly it was done. The entire surface, a circle of water maybe twenty feet in diameter, was solid with boiling, flipping fish, flowing over the corkline in the low places, a very large set.

The men on the seiner leaned back; the men on the carrier began their work. The thick hose was lowered, and in minutes a stream of fish poured into her hold, while a stream of water emptied over the side. From a pipe out of the big dewatering box between the two fish holds gushed a slurry of water and scales— a syrupy, silver fluid pouring into the waiting baskets on deck.

"Eyeshadow," said Henry, the skipper of the Pauline, rolling his eyes and watching the baskets fill. "The scales get used to make eyeshadow and mascara and such."

Pauline filled both holds, 120,000 pounds. We slid in and took another 60,000.

And when we were done loading ourselves, there were *still* fish left. David waved to his men to let the end of the net go, and enough fish to fill yet another carrier swam away slowly into the black water.

"How does he do it?" I asked Henry, just before they threw the lines off and headed across the bay to Rockland. "One set and he loads us both."

"Ah, you mean David," he said. "Now that boy, he's got the touch."

At 2 A.M. we made the harbor; at 5 the first boat was alongside, wanting bait. By 8 our "off the boat" sales were done, and we walked a few hundred yards up Main Street for breakfast before we started delivering the big orders to the lobster dealers.

74

More tired faces were gathered around the table, and Tom filled us in on the night's activities. He had been sitting in a cove in the outboard when the fog rolled in.

"I could hear fish flipping, somewhere *close*, so I went after them; I figured I'd get on top of them before I called anyone. . . . I kept heading toward the noise. Sometimes I'd stop and listen, and then go some more. Each time I'd stop, they'd be off in some new direction, but it was a *big* bunch, you could tell that by the sound. . . . And then I just plain got lost. I thought I was still over by Old Harbor and figured I'd come along the shore to town, just feeling my way along. Then all of a sudden I heard the blast of the horn on Heron Neck—somehow I'd gotten completely turned around, crossed over to the back side of Green's Island. I couldn't hear the fish, and I was afraid of getting lost again, so I just tied onto the first lobster buoy I came to and sacked out on the bottom of the skiff until it got light and the fog scaled off. . . ."

I finished my coffee and stood up; Ann did the same. We strolled outside, fended off the dog, and headed back to the boat. After a few deliveries around the harbor, we'd be done for the day.

A lobsterboat lay alongside Amaretto. A heavy, ruddy-faced man and a boy were helping themselves to our bait; the hole in the pile looked like a good twenty bushels.

"Hullo," he cried out. "No one was around, so we dug out five bush. . . ."

The next night, when Jim had almost given up on them, the fish moved in.

Tom was alone, half dozing in the open skiff, when he woke to a sound like rain on the water and realized it was fish, finning and flipping on the surface all around him—the cove was full of fish at last. So he radioed Jim, and the rest of the crew came. Working with flashlights, and quiet as they could be for fear of scaring the fish, they "ran the twine" and trapped the herring in ten acres of shallow bottom.

Next came the setting of the square "pocket," anchoring its four corners, the whole thing set along the corks of the "running twine," but in a deep hole, the deepest part of the cove.

And finally, the men put heavy weights over the corks between the cove and the pocket, ran back to the harbor in the fog, and called it a night.

In the black of the night, unseen by any eye, in the last hour before dawn, the fish sensed that they were trapped, felt the deeper, safer water outside the net, sought and found the place where the corks were weighted down, and as one, drove over them, only to be trapped again in the little box of net that was the pocket. And in the morning the men came back and hauled the "running twine" back into the dory, and the fish of the night before were neatly trapped, swimming around and around in a little box of net a hundred feet on a side.

Sometimes fish would drive into a cove night after night, each group to be shut off and tricked into a pocket, until there might be four or five pockets of fish in a cove waiting to be sold, waiting for "market."

But for us, the bait business was still hard to figure out. On a perfect morning

"In the evening we steamed to Seal Island."

when every boat in the harbor should have been off the mooring and gone by six, only a few bothered to go.

"Lobsters ain't crawling," was the only explanation I got.

So we slid off to Swan's Island to deliver fifty "bush" I couldn't sell anyplace closer and which I refused to dump. Three hours' steaming, an hour unloading, and another three hours back, hardly breaking even. We got back to Vinalhaven just in time to check the oil, make a few phone calls, and head off down the bay again in case the boys decided the lobsters were crawling next day.

For all their waiting, all their work, Jim's gang got just two boatloads out of their shut-off. Something must have happened. It had looked so good, but there were two "trips" in the pocket and not a bushel more. So far it hadn't been much of a season for Tom and the others in Jim's stop seining gang. Luckily they also purse seined, or the season would have been almost a total pooch.

"Well, after the pilot gets his share, and the guy that owns the twine gets his share, and we divide up what's left six or seven ways . . ." Alton's voice trailed off. I got the point.

And when the plane went up to look again the next night, the fish had "backed off" the shore, and the plane searched around the whole island without seeing a single school.

But the pilot heard of a big school off Popham Beach, fifty miles to the west, a big school and off no one's shore. "Easy money" the pilot told them, so at six in the morning, with high hopes, towing dories and outboards behind them, the Nighthawk was off, over the horizon to the west.

In the evening we steamed to Seal Island and a very different world. After a week away the place was as magic and as powerful as ever. The sun died over the mainland hills twenty miles to the west, and we slid in behind the low island to drop the anchor and wait.

But for a few lobster buoys along the shore, there was no sign of man's existence at all, and when the dusk came the storm petrels swooped around us, filling the night with their soft callings.

Ann went down to the fo'c's'le to sleep, and I lay half awake in the pilothouse bunk, listening to the VHF radio and the faint backwash from the shore close at hand. I knew we were in for a long wait. There were company carriers out there who would be loaded first.

I fell asleep, and awoke deep in the night. The pilothouse had filled with fog from the open doorway, and the radio was silent.

I called Tommy, our seiner that night.

"Ah, we're over to Metinic now. . . . We're still trying to load the fact'ry boat here," he came back to me. His voice seemed hollow and far away. "These fish're quite thin. . . . I'm not sure we'll be able to load you both. . . . Maybe you should give David a call, he's 'round those parts somewhere. . . ."

Metinic was two hours away to the west, and by the time we got there, even if Tommy could set for us, the sky would be showing first light, the fish making their move deeper into the water.

"Hullo. . . ." David answered my call right off. He sounded sleepy; I could hear his engine going full bore in the background. He must have loaded his regular market and been headed for the barn.

77

"Where are you?"

"I dunno. . . . Up the bay somewhere."

"You want to set for me?"

"Ohhhhh . . . I suppose I could disturb the boys' beauty sleep if I saw something. . . ." A long pause, then "What's this?"

"What's what, David?" I could hear his sonar rotating faintly.

"Mnnnn. . . ." Another yawn. "Well, I'll be damned, we just steamed over a bunch. . . . Well, I'd better get 'em up. . . . You could head over this way if you wanted to. How many you want?"

"Load me."

"Ah . . . that's the spirit."

I started the engine up, flipped on the radar, and went forward to haul up the anchor. Around us, above us, was only inky, foggy black. The anchor chain clanking aboard woke Ann and Corn. She stuck her head out the hatch. Beneath her Corn growled.

"What's up?"

"David did it again."

"Did what?"

"Everyone else is still tacking around the bay trying to find fish, and David's already done and headed up the bay. So I called him to see if he wanted to set for us, and bango, he's onto 'em right away."

Then we were steaming, the wet fog sliding past us, and from a dot on the radar screen David became a glow and finally a boat with a net out and four men peering silently into the water.

In every set there is a powerful moment, and it comes right at the very end. Up to that point the fish have only been a target on the sonar screen, a trace on a depth recorder or maybe a flurry in the water. During the set, the net may have ripped, or the fish were too fast or too clever, swimming out the bottom before the net was pursed. So at the end is the waiting, the hauling up of the bottom of the net, seeing what the set will bring.

The water turned in an instant from black to silver, and the fish boiled up between the boats, pushing them apart, and the only sound was that dull, odd roaring of millions of little tails beating against each other and the surface all at once.

Ann worked the winch, and I the long handle of the dipnet. David brought over the usual paper cups, handing me one. He looked quietly down at our load of fish. He seemed immensely tired.

"You haul today, too?" I asked.

He just nodded. He had a lobsterboat, and was one of the best lobstercatchers out of that harbor. I had been told that on days when a big haul would be five or six crates (500 to 600 pounds) of lobsters, David might steam into the harbor, the last boat home, and unload nine or ten. And sometimes when he was lobstering late, out beyond Seal Island, with herring to catch that night, he'd call up his crew and they'd bring the seiner out, and he'd anchor his lobsterboat up behind the island, get on the seiner, and fish herring all night.

He had little to say that night. His eyes looked vacant, burned out, as if he had

78

expended all his energy in finding the fish. Then he was gone, and we were alone in the night and the fog. When we ran up the bay, outside the boat there was nothing—not a ripple or the least swell to make us feel at sea, or even in the water, an eerie sensation. Once I shut off the running lights and stood outside for a moment. Only the dimmest shape of the boat was visible at all, and I was uneasy about getting too close to the rail. I imagined not ocean at all, but a bottomless, limitless void beyond.

We entered the harbor at last, and the fog became even thicker. Finally we just took the boat out of gear, for on the radar we were surrounded by a myriad of targets—boats, wharves—and yet out the window was only wet, black nothingness. I went up to the bow, feeling as though I were in a plane descending out of the overcast, the needles unwinding, the pilots waiting for the runway lights to appear ahead.

Then finally the light on the fish plant wharf emerged from the black, Ann had a line around the pilings, and we were done, the engine shut down and the hollow silence ringing in our ears.

Seven

Morning brought the rare treat of sleep. Thick fog kept most of the lobster fleet in, and our entire load was pretty much committed to the big lobster buyers. We walked uptown for breakfast in a strange, gray world. Pickups crept past with dim yellow spots for lights, and the fog was a robe around us.

At noon, we were eastbound "on instruments" for a lobster buyer "down east," farther northeast along the coast. Three hours we steamed, and for all that time there was nothing but the thick, wet, gray stuff enveloping us. Occasionally a lobster buoy slid past or we got the faintest whiff of spruce or pine as an island passed close aboard. Sometimes when Ann was steering, I'd walk up to the very bow, stick my head out over the water, and listen as we cleaved the sea with our passing. Behind me the pilothouse was the faintest outline and no more.

When it drew back at last, leaving us blinking in the brilliant sunshine, our decks steaming dry, we were in Burnt Coat Harbor on Swan's Island. There were woods and fields right down to the shore, white frame farmhouses, a small settlement, and a lobster co-op.

It was to be an hour before they could unload us, so we hoisted Cornwallis up the dock and walked with the taste and smells of childhood summers all around us—a general store with a big porch, tar bubbles on a hot road, fields stretching away on either side, and Amaretto at the wharf, a postcard from the past. But the dream dissolved into a tedious half day spent unloading dead fish, a bushel at a time, hoisted up over my head, swung into a building, dumped into a barrel, and sent back empty. All the while, bloody fish juice dripped down on top of me where I stood, up to my hip-boot tops in herring in the hold, unable to move.

And when we were done, three hours to unload a hundred and fifty bushels, the manager of the co-op took me around to our stern and pointed at three lobster pot buoys in a cluster, their lines leading down to our propeller.

"Ah . . . the fellas don't really appreciate seeing their gear cut off. Next time, maybe you should stop before you come in here, and cut out anything that you got in there. . . ." He squinted out at the fogbank hanging offshore. "I know you can't always miss 'em, but just don't bring 'em in here." He took a boathook, fished around, hauled in a line and then a lobster pot we had probably towed for a few miles, and set it on the float.

It was a constant problem. In many places where we had to go, the lobster pot buoys were so thick a boat our size could barely maneuver in daylight, much less in the night and fog, without occasionally snaring one.

I put on a ripped wet suit jacket and spent a tedious half hour with the knife, holding my breath, diving down to hold tight to the skeg, and hacking away at the mass of rope around our wheel. And when I climbed out, stripped off the rubber jacket, and stood in the hot sun of that windless July day, it was a full

81

hour before I could stop my violent shivering—a sobering reminder of what awaited a misstep, a wrong turn on deck as we steamed.

We started up, and steamed for Vinalhaven. Outside the harbor, the sunny warmth of the early evening died as Amaretto entered the wall of fog that had retreated from the shore but a few hundred yards. Then came another three hours of tedious running, with nothing beyond the windows but swirling gray, until at last I slowed, took Amaretto out of gear, and waited for the fish plant wharf to appear out of the murk, and we fell quickly into an exhausted sleep.

In the morning, in the coffee shop, the Popham Beach story:

"We only pooched about $20,000 worth of boss' very best twine," Tom told us bitterly, "and didn't get fish one out of the deal."

The plane had seen the fish on the sandy bottom right off the beach, and called down for them to set the net quick or miss them.

So they laid the long net out, but as soon as it was all set the pilot called down again, "Haul it back, the fish are going out around the end. There's an even better spot down the beach. That's no good there. . . ." And then he was gone, winging his way inland, low on fuel.

Before they had even begun to pull the immense wall of net back into the dories, the tide change brought a swell, a swell with no wind, from a distant storm. It heaped up steeply against the current running from the mouth of the Kennebec River, and in minutes it was too rough to work. They towed the dories and the outboards up inside the river, tied up all the boats, and came down to the beach to watch.

The leadline on the bottom of the net "sanded in," became embedded in the soft sandy bottom, and then the breakers from the big swell did their work. They ripped the net slowly apart, sending the corks and the lines ashore and leaving the leads and half the twine on the bottom. For two days they watched tourists picking up the corks on the beach, claiming them as souvenirs.

So they gave it up, and steamed the ten hours back to Vinalhaven empty-handed. In their absence a large body of fish had been spotted close to home, and from the east and west poachers and herring rustlers had come to find what they had gone to seek: a school of herring, and an unclaimed cove to fish them in.

For up and down the coast, the herring season had been poor, and many sensed the windy fall, the lean months ahead. A single night's work, a single shut-off if the weather and the market were right, a single good school of fish swimming in at the right time, could make a season.

The patriarch of the herring stop-seine fishery on Vinalhaven was an older man who no longer fished but owned most of the dories and twine. He contented himself with telling the men where to fish and coordinating the selling when they made a shut-off. He was visibly angry at the sight of fishermen from other areas snooping around the coves he had always assumed were his alone.

"A dory in every cove," he said in his hoarse voice to Jim. And so, from barns and sheds all over the island came dories that hadn't seen the water in years.

Their seams gaped too wide to be caulked, so they were dragged down to the shore, launched with Styrofoam blocks for flotation, and towed off to mark another cove for the Vinalhaven boys, to keep away the interlopers.

Starry darkness found David and me, five miles from the nearest land, our heads down, watching the pool of water between the boats, waiting.

Then it was all fish, beating the water with their fins. But something was different, and I looked and instead of bright herring, what surfaced were

"Thick fog kept most of the lobster fleet in."

83

mackerel, beautiful, slim fifteen-inch creatures—tinkers, they were called around these parts.

I looked up at David, unsure of what to do. The wheels in my head were turning, thinking of the Boston market and of fifty cents a pound, the fish trapper's price.

David shrugged, and motioned for his crew to stop drying up the fish. They let the net back a bit into the water, giving the fish room so they wouldn't smother and die while I decided what to do.

"We can set again if you want."

But I shook my head, and picked one of the fish out of the net. Beautiful, silver-green, fresh and firm-fleshed, it seemed a shame to sell such a creature for bait.

So we gambled and took a "trip," a boatload, steaming westward to Matinicus Island and the nearest telephone to find a mooring in the still harbor, wait for the morning, arrange for a truck and ice to meet us on the mainland, and perhaps sell the smallest amount for bait.

Five A.M.: a bright, clear morning, and the bump of a boat alongside. I pulled on my clothes, stumbled out on deck. A young lobstercatcher was looking at the mackerel.

"I'll take eight bush."

We swung them over to him. They were perfect, still sweet smelling and firm. I said it'd be forty-two bucks.

But instead the kid threw off his lines, started up, and moved away from us without paying.

He said, "Well, you're on my mooring, too, so I guess we'll call it good." Then he gave it full throttle and headed out of the harbor and away, throwing spray wide.

By eight o'clock the tide was up enough and we maneuvered through the very narrow harbor to lay at the wharf. We walked past a ramshackle collection of vehicles to the little general store. Matinicus has no regular ferry service; once a vehicle makes it there, such things as registration and inspections become less important than in other places.

The phone connection to Boston was scratchy, the fish broker unimpressed. Outside, the sun rose higher and higher in the sky, and our thirty thousand dollar score began to look like a trip to the fish meal plant.

"Yeah, well, call me back this afternoon. Maybe by then I'll have found someone who wants 'em. . . ." I slammed the phone down, swore, and headed out the door to the harbor. We had 'em, now we had to peddle 'em.

The local lobster buyer was out of bait and the boats were lined up; I persuaded him to take a hundred and fifty bush of "macs."

"Good 'spear-ons,'" I told him, a "spear-on" being the local term for any fresh-caught bait, generally fish large enough to be speared onto a baiting iron rather than stuffed into a bait bag.

So with Ann on the bow, buoy bag fender in hand to push us off the boats in that tiny, crowded harbor, we worked Amaretto alongside the float and started basketing out the mackerels.

84

". . . the beautiful fish we had taken and sold for bait and fish meal."

85

"Yeah, let's see now, that's nine hundred bucks for those hundred and fifty bushels, and ah, oh yeah . . . see that kid over there?" The boat of the kid who had fleeced us that morning was just visible out past the breakwater.

The lobster dealer squinted in the morning sun for a moment.

"Yeah, that's Irwin's kid. . . ."

"Yeah, well, he got ten bushels this morning early, said he didn't have any cash, but that you could pay me and settle up with him later . . . take it off his lobsters." Ann looked over at me, a grin starting on her face. "So that makes it nine sixty."

The man nodded, peeling the greenbacks off a thick roll, and we were done.

Then it was work our way slowly out the way we had come before the dropping tide stranded us. When we were out of that rocky hole and steaming up the bay, I turned the wheel over to Ann and got on the radio, called the marine operator, and talked to all the lobster buyers, cajoling them into trying a few mackerel for a change. We traveled north, then east, selling a hundred here, fifty there, whatever we could peddle, ending finally at North Haven, a picturesque summer community with fine houses set on both sides of a tree-lined channel. Curious men in blazers and women in skirts came to look down at us as we lay at the bait scow, unloading those beautiful fish. But in the end we still had a third of a trip left, and what would have been perfect fish for breakfast, for freezing, for smoking, or just hawking by the roadside had lost their color and firmness and swirled around dully in a pool of bloody water at the bottom of the fish hold.

With heavy hearts we headed across the bay to the fish meal plant in Rockland, where a huge, filthy hose sucked us dry.

We washed and scrubbed the boat again and again to get the smell of the fish meal plant off, and then Tom, who had come along to help, borrowed a truck and took us to dinner overlooking the harbor at Camden, a few miles away to the north. It was as different from Vinalhaven as night is from day. There wasn't a lobsterboat to be seen—only yachts, and in the streets, boutiques, real estate offices, and gift shops.

I drank and felt crummy about the day, about the beautiful fish we had taken and sold for bait and fish meal. I wished that we had let them go instead. Tom and Ann steered Amaretto back across the bay in the black, and I lay on the foredeck, looking up at the stars and wondering at the chain of circumstances that had brought me to that curious end.

A few days later, in the dark of the moon, a large body of herring that three different gangs had been watching finally moved into Robert's Harbor, one of Jim's coves, and he was there to shut the door on them.

In the afternoon, Ann and I slid by in the Amaretto and inquired about getting a load of fish from the shut-off, to save us an all-night chase around the bay. We were surprised that there were no other carriers at the shut-off, taking out fish.

"We haven't got any market." Jim stood in the Nighthawk with Tom and the others. In the pockets, four neat little squares of fish and twine, the water was dark with perhaps twenty or thirty thousand bushels of fish swimming around and around.

"They got sixes shut off to west'ard, and now they don't want these fives. . . ." Fives and sixes were the number of fish that could be packed to a standard can. The larger the number, the smaller the fish.

"Any chance of getting a trip?"

No one looked too enthusiastic. They were still hoping to find some market right off. It was about the same amount of work to load us as it was a big company carrier, and we paid a lot less.

"Maybe tomorrow. Maybe we'll have a boat by then, and we can load you at the same time. We're still calling around for market."

So we anchored, Tom came aboard to visit, and we ate and drank and one by one fell asleep on the deck in the hot sun with the cries of the gulls circling over the pocket loud in our ears.

The sun dropped in the sky and the day died in the west and finally we woke up, and still no boats came for Jim's fish. We let Tom off to wait and watch for more fish in the night, and we steamed off again to the south'ard, to find someone to load us.

In the morning, one of the lobster dealers told us about trying to sell herring in the old days: "Fifty cents a bushel we got, and we had to wait two months to get that." The speaker, a handsome man of sixty-five, paused a moment from layering the salt onto the bait we were passing him. He bought lobsters and sold bait from a little float in the harbor, but in years gone by had fished herring all around the island.

"Muriel took those fish, six days in a row, a full trip every day she took, steamed all the way to North Lubec, and was back to get another trip the next day on the tide. Six days in a row she did that. She was the fastest carrier on the coast then."

On our way around to the east side to deliver, we passed Robert's Harbor again and the boys' shut-off. *Another* school had come in the night and they shut them off, put them in still *another* pocket. But still, the soonest the cannery could send their boats was a week away.

When there were canneries up and down the coast, there were thousands of cutters—women that worked with scissors, trimming the herring, putting them into cans. Then when the foreign fleets came and the herring disappeared, the canneries closed, and the women often found better, easier work. And now, when at last a few more fish had come back to the coast, the canneries couldn't find enough women to pack the fish and were forced to operate at reduced capacity.

August came in hot and still. The pace of our work grew even more frantic. We had eight, ten weeks at the most to pay off our bills and make our winter money. Days passed in a blur of loading and unloading, a meal snatched here, a few hours of sleep there.

On a rare day when we were done early, we took the outboard to Brimstone, a wild mountaintop of an island, steep, grassy, the few trees twisted and stunted by the wind. We set out the blankets and food on a beach of shiny smooth stones.

"In the pockets, four neat little squares of fish and twine, the water was dark with perhaps twenty or thirty thousand bushels of fish swimming around and around."

To the north and to the west were the approaches to Vinalhaven, looking that low-tide afternoon like an impassable mass of reefs and breakers.

It was said that when a great storm was coming, all the halibut up and down the bay would come to the beach and swallow the stones, to sink to the bottom until the gale had passed. For humans, the stones were said to bring good luck. Carried in a pocket, to be taken out from time to time and rubbed against one's cheek, they would grow sleek and shiny with the skin oils.

The sun began to fall in the sky, and we headed back in the outboard, but halfway to the harbor there was something in the water, and we stopped. At first we thought it might be a whale, its tail tangled in a lobster pot buoy. But then we looked closer and saw the baleful eye and languid movement of the ocean sunfish, one of the oddest creatures to swim off those shores. At five or six hundred pounds, it was a giant saucer of flesh and bones wallowing beneath the surface, half awash, watching us carefully—an eerie, spooky sight. Its only natural defense, it is said, is the foul taste of its flesh.

But seen just then, from a skiff on a late afternoon, a cold wind making up, a fin poking above the surface and a huge cold eye staring at us from below, it seemed mysterious, and somehow sinister.

And when night came, full dark and windy, it was the four of us again, Amaretto, Ann, Cornwallis and I, jogging bow up in the seaway at Matinicus Roads, a wide channel between Criehaven to the south and Matinicus to the north. David was out there somewhere, only a shape on the radar screen, watching a bunch of fish, biding his time, waiting for just the right moment and he would have them.

Ann took the wheel and sent me below to the fo'c's'le, where the kerosene lamp was lit, dinner was on the table, and the dog snuggled against my feet. There were even flowers in a little bud vase, but how very different was the world outside when I was done and slid the hatch back: wind, water, cold, and black.

Then David lit up and called us in. Spotlight on, we proceeded gingerly, for a good sea was running, the wind coming on strong. I rigged the biggest fenders and Ann put on her parka and went up to the bow to throw the line.

The pressure to come in just right was a tangible thing—the wind, the seas could easily push the boats together, the net could foul my propeller, and we could get into a jam, a "jackpot." I felt my heart in my throat as we slid slowly in, my hand on the spotlight control, picking up the edge of the corkline, David's boat rising and falling, the tense, waiting men.

Then we were in, trying to tie the corks to our rail. But they were too heavy. Even working together, Ann and I couldn't get them high enough, so two of David's strong men came aboard, lent their backs to the effort, and it was done.

When the fish came up, I saw at once that it was a very big set, many boatloads for us, bigger than any I had ever seen. We dried the net up partway, just enough so we could dip out what we needed, the live fish wriggling and flipping in our hold, the rest swimming round and round, so they could be set free alive.

But something happened beneath us in the net after we had begun to brail. The mass of fish held the boats apart in the seaway, but the strain on the lines and corks suddenly increased, and both boats began to heel toward each other as if there were a very great weight pulling the net and us down together. David's rail began to creak with the strain, and meshes in the net began ripping with sharp little pops.

He was at the rail watching as the boats heeled over more and more, his rail almost in the water. At the very last moment he waved, and his crew began letting twine out, back over the rail, and the crisis eased. After a long while the boats came upright and we could take the twine back and load herring again.

We loaded ourselves to the very top, both hatches full, the fish flowing out over the decks, the boat low in the water. David waved to his men and they let the twine back out. The corks on the top of the net immediately sank, staying underwater as perhaps a hundred tons of herring swam away into the night.

I yelled over to him, asking what had happened in the net when the boats started to heel over.

"Fish," he yelled back, and made a motion with his hands like a big bunch of fish swimming straight down. With the fish gone, the wind pressed the boats together, and the lines were quickly off. His gang pushed our bow clear of their rigging as we backed away. Then we were alone in the black, and we steamed past Wooden Ball Island, No Man's Land and finally up the bay for home, the wind rising all the time, the phosphorescent seas sliding past us. Ann made her way forward and below, and I was left to think about David—of all the fish that he seemed to catch so effortlessly when no one else could find any, and the irony of not being able to sell more than a small portion of them.

As opposed to many other fisheries, the Maine herring fishery was "market limited," in the sense that the fleet could catch far more than the buyers could handle. Whereas David had the vessel and the skill to load many carriers almost any night, the industry had shrunk drastically in recent years, and it was a rare night that he had "market" or buyers for more fish than he could catch. Many nights, he had no one to buy his fish at all. Even the big Pauline, David's regular market, would usually take half a load; the cannery just wasn't capable of handling any more.

He had a few dories of twine in the harbor for stop seining, and his own coves to watch, but his heart wasn't in it. He liked the chase, I had been told, the nights down the bay in his seiner.

We slid over to Matinicus when we were done, for the lobster buyer was out of bait again. When daylight came the usual lobsterboats came alongside, and I recognized one of the men as another of the players in the herring game, the owner of a seiner.

"Discount . . . gimmee a discount," he said, in a peculiar, high-pitched voice.

I looked around the harbor. Other lobsterboats were lined up waiting for our bait, and the lobster dealer's bait floats were riding high up out of the water, empty. The Bay Lady was off to the east'ard. It was a seller's market.

"Six bucks, buddy, take it or leave it."

I knew the man: shady, but likeable. On a less busy morning I might have haggled with him, but I was tired. It had been a long night, and we'd had maybe two hours' sleep after getting in.

Something thumped on my deck. "Now, I'll give you that nice lobster, and you give me that bait for five bucks."

I looked down. A "jumbo" or oversized lobster was crawling across my deck toward me, holding up a huge claw. The whole thing must have weighed ten or eleven pounds, a monster.

"And it was a weary and discouraged gang that got out their little seine and caught a thousand bushels of fine herring to sell as lobster bait."

91

Gingerly I picked it up, dropped it over the side, and watched it disappear toward the bottom. They were illegal to keep or have; they were prime breeders, and the dwindling lobster population needed them.

"Let's go, pal, six bucks. I got customers waiting." I made as if to throw his tie-up line back.

Finally he sighed, and opened his empty bait barrels. We swung him what he needed and he reluctantly opened his fat wallet and passed over the crisp bills. Then he spoke again.

"How many did David have in that set, anyway?"

I told him.

"How does he do it? The rest of us have to scratch away the whole night . . . and he finds fish wherever he looks." He shook his head, and moved off toward the harbor mouth.

The next day five huge Canadian carriers came from the east—from Grand Manan, Campobello, and Saint Andrews, New Brunswick, where there were no fish just then and the canneries were desperate for them. The broad, deep boats with unfamiliar names slid around to Robert's Harbor to inspect the hundreds of tons of herring Jim had swimming around in the pockets.

But they wanted big fish instead of the perfect smaller ones, and sailed away to the west, and it was a weary and discouraged gang that got out their little seine and caught a thousand bushels of fine herring to sell as lobster bait, all they could sell of the twenty or thirty thousand they had shut off, a good part of a year's money for every man there, if only they could sell them.

In the night, a storm from the southeast; in the morning the ledges beyond the harbor were white, and a heavy swell drove into the harbor, working Amaretto up and down against the pilings.

Even the ferry stayed in, and pickup after pickup would cruise along the shore road and park for a moment while anxious men would look down the bay at the sea churning up the ledges and wonder about their lobster pots, or their fish in pockets in coves all around the island. The storm was fierce, unexpected, an October blow in August.

"They lost 'em, they lost 'em all, the twine was bad, and now the cannery just called and said they'd take the fish, all that they could get. . . ." Ann brought the news, shaking her head, sad for all of them.

And evening found us sitting on a little bench by the edge of the harbor, eating burgers and fries from the takeout stand, looking out at the sea. The wind had let go, the afternoon had turned warm, the storm had gone. Once again, it looked like a "chance."

The gale had changed everything—had churned up the coast, driven thousands of lobster pots ashore, burst the nets holding many boatloads of fish—and as we watched, three company carriers slid into the harbor one after the other: it would be a purse seine evening.

So in shorts and T-shirts, Ann and I threw off the lines and joined the procession, out of the harbor, down the bay. The sea replaced the land, the dark replaced the light. The ocean air was cool and damp; we changed into long pants, flannel shirts, ready for whatever the night would bring.

92

Eight

Seal Island: sunset and evening star. Four dories in the cove, five men around a fire, a plane in the air, and a radio talking in a tinny voice:

". . . Yeah, I don't know, Jim, they're not moving in yet, least not that I can see. There's still a good bunch maybe a mile south, just hanging there. Maybe they'll move in after dark or maybe tomorrow. . . ."

The plane swooped low over the cove, dipped its wings, and then it was away and climbing off to the north and the dim line of Vinalhaven on the horizon.

A long while passed. No one said anything. Finally one of the men stood up.

"Well, maybe I'll get some sleep for a change, too," he yawned, and headed over the boulders and bushes to a blue tent. "You 'kin wake me if you see anything, Jim."

I stood up too, and made my way slowly up the rough slope behind the campsite, up toward the very ridge of the island. Tom, Ann, and the others stayed by the fire, watching Jim walk down to the shore and the outboard boat.

As I walked, the land and the bushes and the grasses ahead of me erupted in birds, crying out, not used to man, not used to being disturbed. The island was a wild place, man a stranger, the rare interloper. It was the nesting place for colony after colony of seabirds, on the cliffs, in the bushes, in the very earth itself in little bird-made hollows.

I found a place to lie at the very top of the ridge, the backbone of the island. The bay spread out before me, and beyond, on the horizon but faintly seen, was the distant twinkle of the mainland towns.

The men had come to camp, and to wait for a big school of fish to come ashore. The pilot had seen them offshore, and this would be the second night of waiting. Ann and I had come, too, for the island fascinated us, and it was a chance to spend some time there between bait trips.

Below me, the sound of an outboard starting up: Jim was going to circle the island, looking with the depth finder, for sometimes the fish could come in after dark.

The sound faded away, then came again, below me and a little to the east, as Jim slowly worked his way around the south side of the island, the skiff creeping in close to the cliffs. I could hear the queer echo of the engine off the sheer rock face.

The light in the sky died away completely, and of the boat below there was nothing but the orange blips of the sounding machine, a faint phosphorescent wake behind. Two hours he searched for fish, but found only hard, empty bottom.

Finally he gave it up, the engine coughed to a halt, and in the sudden stillness

94

there was the faint swish of the oars and the thunk of a punt hitting the beach.

And then I saw something. Off to the south, the faintest glow in the water, the thinnest image in the black. I skinned my eyes and looked again, hard as I could. For a while there was nothing, but at last I saw it again, a little brighter, pulsing, something moving beneath the surface of the water, like the school of fish I had seen with Junior that chill evening in Christmas Cove. Except this was bigger. Dimmer, but definitely bigger, perhaps what the plane had seen, a very large school of fish making the phosphorescence of the water fire with its passing.

There was something else, too, off to the east, a long way out, two, maybe three miles. It looked like four or five spots of light, very dim and indistinct. I watched a long while and thought they were whales, a school of humpbacks probably, moving in from offshore, like the herring making the water glow with their passing. They seemed to be moving toward the island.

Finally I stumbled down to the skiff, made my way out to Amaretto in the darkness, and savored an exhausted, dreamless sleep.

In the morning the smoke from the breakfast fire rose straight and high into the still air.

We hauled our anchor, traveled two hours to the northwest, and unloaded the last of our fish in North Haven. It was a tapestry of color and rich detail, of yachts and of people, houses on the shore, sailboats in the channel. And yet for all that, it was but a pale shadow of the beauty of the place from which we had come.

Seal Island had been sky and water, a campfire, men in tattered sweaters and vests drinking coffee and looking out at their string of dories off a rocky beach, a still and magic place. Without ever saying it to each other, Ann and I wanted the same thing—to get done unloading, clean up, and get away, back to the island.

It was as if what we had found out there, miles from any inhabited land, was a rare and precious thing, and that we might return and find it changed.

Seal Island: early evening, cool, a campfire, four dories in the cove below, the sense of a faraway outpost, as if instead of paperbacks the men might have held whalebones, carving scrimshaw.

"Before the war, my grandfather fished down here and used the island as a fish camp, summers."

We were walking along the shore, Ann, Tom, myself, and one of the other herring fishermen from Vinalhaven. We passed a place with a few bleached timbers still jammed into the rocks. Peter, the other man, stopped for a moment, looking around.

"And there was supposed to be a spring around here, too. His camp was here, these timbers were his. . . ."

"He still talks about those days an awful lot. Grandma was with them, and they had a garden spot. They'd only go into town every two weeks or so, unless he had a big jag of lobsters to sell. My dad told me it was always the best part of the year for them, those months out here."

95

He went on to say that all the other uninhabited islands had little fish camps in those days, for the boats were slower, and didn't allow the men to fish the islands and run home each night.

And they watched for the herring. There were no spotter planes in those days, and no sounders or fish finders for little boats. It was just a matter of going out each evening, rowing around the cove in a skiff, putting the sounding pole down into the water, and feeling for the herring.

"My dad always told me about the big one. One night in the middle of July my grandfather shook him awake. 'Listen,' grandfather said, and from inside the little cabin you could hear it—fish flipping in the night, a rustling, a roaring, a sound like nothing he had ever heard before.

"So they took the skiff, and my dad told me he put his *hand* in the water and felt the fish, swimming, hitting his hand.

"My grandfather rowed the dory and my father set out the twine, easing the leads and corks over so they wouldn't make a noise and scare the fish. And more men came out from town to help them and the weather stayed good and they got the fish out. A week straight they loaded fish. It was that big a shut-off. . . ."

It was the war that changed it all, he said. The government made the island into a bombing range. It was perfect for that—uninhabited, far from anything else. The fishermen were just squatters anyway. For years, no one could go there, and when the planes came you could hear the thud of the bombs. If it was night, the people from Vinalhaven, the people that had fished Seal Island, would stand on a hill and look across the ten miles of water and see the flash of the exploding bombs, watch the planes make their runs.

Even after the bombing stopped, no one went ashore. There was danger from unexploded bombs. Finally the government made it into a wildlife refuge, and for the first time the men went back. They went just to walk around and see what the years had brought, for they all had faster boats then, and there was no real reason to camp on the island when they could fish it and still be in their own beds at night.

At first the island was scarred and wasted, with great holes and craters in the land from the bombs and the shells. But nature and time are great healers, and after a while vegetation covered the wounds, and finally even the birds came back.

"But the fish never came back. That was the funny thing. Even when we weren't allowed to go on the island, we'd come back summer nights to watch for herring when they might be around. And they never did return. No one really knew why. Maybe it was the bombing, shaking up the bottom or something. It's just these last couple of years that the fish have started to move in closer here. Maybe this'll be the year they finally come back. . . ."

We were at the easternmost point. We had a view of the two wide bights that were the north side of the island, and the wide ocean on all sides.

"Look." Ann pointed. "There, aren't those whales? They look like they're heading over here."

She was right. There was a pod of humpbacks in the distance, moving slowly, ponderously—breathing, lifting their tails high, and sounding, diving deep beneath the surface. They seemed to be traveling toward Seal Island.

From the northern horizon, a dot slowly rose, circled, and moved around the distant island that was the home of all the men there. The plane was up. It was time to get back to the dories. We stood up together and began walking the shore toward the camp, the boats, and the other men.

The sun touched the horizon.

The men were in the small boats and the dories, listening to the pilot talking. He was just south of the island then, headed back over the cove again for a last look before heading up the bay. Suddenly, fifty yards from Amaretto, there was a commotion. As if by magic, hundreds of herring jumped clear of the water, hanging there for an instant. There was just time for us to turn our heads, to wonder what had caused the odd sight, when the water opened again, and a whale climbed after them, its cavernous mouth open, capturing half of them in an instant, then sliding back into the water to disappear with a tremendous splash. The whole thing took maybe four seconds. We sat there too stunned to speak.

Then, clearly over the water in the still evening, every word sharp, the pilot, the walkie-talkie, speaking frantically, rapidly:

"Jesus Christ, Jim, you see that? Those goddamn whales are herding those fish into the cove. They're *herding* them. Get your end ready, this might be the big one we've waited for all summer!"

The plane was above the cove, engine throttled right back, steeply banked, circling, dropping lower and lower, the pilot looking down, watching it all. And on the water, a frenzy of activity, outboards starting up, men scrambling over dories piled high with nets.

Jim towed one dory to the rocky beach at the edge of the cove, scrambled ashore to a boulder the size of a house, made a line fast around it, brought the end of it back to the dory, and tied it off to the very end of the net. And as we looked out over the cove we could see little patches of disturbed water, maybe an acre or two at a time, ripples, as millions of fish pushed up, their backs and fins on the surface, while the whales slowly herded them in to where the men waited. The whales spouted and moved back and forth. Between them and the shore was a large school of fish, larger than any I had yet seen.

Jim was in the outboard boat, waiting, watching for his moment. When the school was in the cove, he would draw the wall of net across. Even aboard Amaretto we sensed the passage of a great body of fish. Beyond him, along the shore fish finned, flipping out of water, dozens in the air at once. It was time. He started up the outboard, waved to the man in the dory, and moved out from shore, the net spilling out behind, the man in the dory clearing the tangles as he set it.

"Hey, HEY, what are you doing?" Dave was on the walkie-talkie, angry. The plane dropped out of the sky, buzzing Jim low. He chopped the engine and yelled out the window and on the walkie-talkie all at once.

"Wait, WAIT, those fish are still coming in. Hold on a bit. You're only making a thousand bucks every minute you wait."

Reluctantly, it seemed, Jim slowed the skiff. The dory stopped in the water, and the net sagged back in toward the shore. Except for the plane there was silence again. Then, slowly, a new sound, like wind or the rushing of faraway water. We looked and saw it—the cove—six or eight acres of water and the entire surface moving with fish.

It was the big one, the shut-off everyone had talked about. Yet there was something awesome about it too, in that moment before Jim ran the twine. I had never seen so many fish before, and it didn't seem possible that they could be caught so easily, by a few men and a couple dories full of net.

The radio spoke, the outboard started again, and slowly a line of white corks appeared behind the dory, making a wide arc across the cove, enclosing maybe five acres of water—a fence of net with corks on top and leads on the bottom, resting on the sandy bottom of the cove. In a few minutes it was done. The net was set, the fish trapped. The plane circled one last time, and there was the face of a man grinning, two fingers held out the window in the victory sign, and then he was gone, throttle forward, headed up the bay for the landing strip in the woods before the light left the sky.

The men worked into the night. The net had to be anchored against the tide, the shore lines wrapped so they wouldn't chafe with the surge against the rocks. Old pieces of twine had to be led ashore onto the rocks so the fish couldn't sneak out by following the shore. When it was all done, we went ashore. Someone stoked up the fire and we all looked out at the night. Jim was the last to come. He had been aboard his boat, using the radio to call the cannery and tell them about the fish. The sooner they could send their boats, the better, for the cove was exposed, and the wrong wind would collapse the twine against the shore.

"Sunday morning," was all he said. It was Friday, and the canneries didn't pack over the weekends, so we had to hold the fish two nights and a day.

"He shouldn't have shut off so much." It was one of the herring fishermen, beside me at the fire.

"How come?"

"Hard to handle a big bunch like that. Jim was right, trying to shut them off when he did. That was a plenty big bunch even then. That pilot's got dollar signs for eyes, and he still doesn't understand that you can shut off too many. They get wild, and you can't handle them. They'll burst a net just by the sheer weight of 'em."

We sat in silence. The night grew very dark, moonless, the fire died down to coals, and we all moved a little closer.

Then, in the cove below, the show started.

At first it was just the dimmest glow, the fish stirring the phosphorescence. But after a while the night grew darker, and the patterns of light below us, brighter. It was, as all had said, a huge school. At times it seemed as if the whole cove was alive, glowing, pulsing, moving, bright and dark, changing all the time. It was unexpected, powerful, and none could remember seeing anything like it in their years of herring fishing. Some said it was the size of the school, others that the water always fired brightest out there, but all watched, spellbound.

The school would gather itself into a brightly glowing, compact bunch, maybe an acre of solid fish. It would creep along the shore, exploring it carefully, looking for a way out—there could be no other explanation. At the ends of the net, where the men had put leaders right onto the rocks, the glowing light in the water would pause for a long time, as if checking it out, deciding what to do next. Then it would slowly proceed outward, along the corkline. They would be on the surface at first, and then the cove would go dark but for a dim light fifty feet down; the fish were on the bottom, feeling there too for a way out.

Then the body seemed to break up, and the water grew dark except for a few scattered flashes here and there. One by one most of the men said their good nights and headed back to the tents. Finally it was just Tom, Ann, myself, and Cornwallis, sitting by what was left of the fire, a blanket thrown over our legs. A long while passed, and I began to doze off.

"Hey, look." Tom poked me awake, pointing down into the cove.

The dim scattered glow of the fish was coalescing again. From here and there, from all the corners of the cove, came glowing clouds of light, merging together, getting bigger, glowing brighter, the whole school forming a single, tight body.

And more: as we watched, the school got even more compact, pulsing brightly with phosphorescence. It moved to the very head of the cove, the farthest point from the net, crowding right back into the rocks. Then suddenly, with a speed that made us catch our breaths, it drove forward to the middle of the net, to a point between two anchors, the weakest point. The fish boiled and pushed against the corkline, and it sagged way out between the anchors. Again and again the fish would regroup, swim back to the rear of the cove, and try again, each time going for the same place, the weakest point.

"All eyes, the first thing after opening, were on the cove below the tents, where something like a breeze played across the water behind the corkline."

99

And each time, a few bushels would spill out over the corks, pushed by the sheer pressure of the fish below. The escaped fish would stay close, swimming back and forth on the other side of the net, a little twinkling, sparkling, cloud in the inky night, as if calling to the huge body of fish behind.

Then the tide began to run, and we could see the entire curve of the net glowing as the current strained through it.

For an hour or more we watched the show, the great school of fish driving against the net, more and more frantically, as if they finally sensed that they were truly trapped, that there was no way out but through the net.

And still the net held. We were lucky. It was about the last good piece of gear left after the Popham Beach fiasco. If they had tried to use any of the older gear, it would have burst long before.

It was deep in the night before Ann and I made it back out to the boat, and even then, after she turned in, I went up on the bow to watch the powerful show in the cove.

Morning came cloudless and still. All eyes, the first thing after opening, were on the cove below the tents, where something like a breeze played across the water behind the corkline. Yet the water beyond, up the bay and as far as the eye could see, was glassy still, unrippled. It was no wind on the cove, but restless fish.

Jim and another were already up, cruising in the outboard boat, checking the ends of the net for chafing where it went ashore, checking the anchor lines where they were made fast to the net, and finally, when they had made sure all was well, just patrolling back and forth in the skiff, looking at the sounding machine, looking at the fish on the chart paper.

When he returned, he brought a strip of the paper with him.

"Still there," he reported to the waiting men, drinking coffee around the fire. "Most of 'em are laying deep, right on the bottom, but it's the big one all right, maybe forty, fifty thousand bushels. . . ." He passed the strip of paper around and all the men looked at the heavy gray smudge along the dark line of the bottom, and there were murmurs and excited talk.

Forty thousand bushels was over a hundred and fifty thousand dollars, thirty or forty boatloads for the big carriers.

Midday: warmer, T-shirt weather. From Vinalhaven, lobsterboats arrived, with families, more tents, boxes of food, kids, cases of beer. There was much to celebrate. The season had been a thin one, after a string of lean years before that. The herring had stayed away from this part of the coast, and now it seemed they might be coming back. It would mean new trucks, maybe boats for the men, washing machines, color TV's for the women, and more.

Now and again Jim would take some of the newcomers in the skiff, over the corkline and into the cove, and cruise slowly, and all would look into the sounder and comment on the mass of fish laying on the bottom, thick beneath the whole cove, barely stirring, just waiting for the darkness and another frenzied chance at freedom. He had the sounding pole in the skiff, and he would pass it to the others, and they would push it down into the water, each one, and hold it, feeling the fish below, and nod or say nothing.

100

But there was concern, too, for it was a very large school. No one there had handled such a big one before. When the time came to set the small seine and herd the fish to the pump, it must be done gingerly, or the fish would spook and go into a mad frenzy, and the net wouldn't hold.

Evening: Distant stars, and a great bonfire, timbers, driftwood heaped into a great pile, roaring, popping, sending great sheets of sparks into the sky. Food spread on wide driftwood planks, cases of beer, the kids playing, the older folks watching, talking, thinking of the great bonanza that swam around in the cove below them. Tomorrow the sardine carriers would come. The timing was just right, the companies were hungry for fish, and they were sending all their boats.

The women looked at catalogs together in the firelight, the men stood together, arms akimbo, looking out at the night, the boats, the cove, the fish. Out on one of the points there was the pop of firecrackers, the distant sound of laughter.

Slowly the fire died, the evening air grew cool, and the people moved closer together, closer to the fire. The last color went from the western sky, and in the cove below the lights began moving in the dark.

The crowd stilled, stared. Few had seen such a thing before. It was what the three of us had seen late the night before, but even more intense. First the flickers of light from all corners of the cove coming together in the center,

"But there was concern, too, for it was a very large school."

coalescing into a tight, brightly glowing cloud, thousands of tons of fish milling tightly, nose to tail, and beyond, shimmering slightly in the tidal current, the net, clearly visible, a necklace, a shimmering curtain across the cove.

Next a murmuring in the crowd and then an audible gasp when, for the first time, the great body of fish drove as one for the net, as if they could sense that in the morning the boats would come and they would begin to die. They hit the net in the weakest part, between the two anchor lines, and it bulged way out. The crowd waited, afraid, but the net held, and just a few bushels escaped over the corkline.

Again the mass of fish drifted back to the farthest corner of the cove, regained its strength and mass, pulsed brighter and brighter as they pushed closer and closer together. Finally they drove forward again and the watchers gasped and the net bulged and held and everyone breathed easy.

It grew late, but the watchers were spellbound. Their lives and those of their parents before them were wrapped up with schools of herring such as this. But never before had there been this—the clear sense of a prey trapped, frantically trying to escape. And something else: this school that they had trapped was larger than any they had seen before. But there was intelligence in it. Anyone who watched could not escape that conclusion.

Finally the show in the cove dimmed. People drifted back to the tents and the boats. Of the fire, there remained only coals.

"Look up here." It was Ann. I followed her up between the boulders dimly seen in the starlight, beyond the tents, up to the ridge, where the land fell away steeply to the sea below. Tom was up there, staring out at something away to the east.

"Over there. See it?"

I looked where he pointed, and finally saw them—faint glowing shapes, bigger than dots, slowly moving in toward the island.

"What d'ya make of it?"

"Whales."

We looked for a long time. They were the ones I had seen two nights before. I was sure of it.

"Kinda odd they're coming back," Tom said. "They disappeared after they ran those fish into the cove. Queer doings, I call it. . . ."

I looked down toward the cove. The fire was just a red circle, but in the cove below, the glowing line of the net was clearly visible, and behind it, the pulsing glow of the fish. I looked over toward the whales again. Tom was right, they were definitely headed toward the cove and the fish. They moved slowly, and we watched them for a long time. For some reason they raised goose bumps up and down my back. Finally, late, in the black, we went back out to Amaretto. We passed close by the net, and the fish glowed and twitched visibly as we passed.

Deep in the night, something woke me up, and I went out on deck. It was very dark; the sky had clouded over. But the water was firing brilliantly, my anchor line clearly outlined in the tide. And then, out beyond the net in the cove, I saw the odd thing. I was about to hit the bunk again, for the night air was cool on my skin, but there was something out there. It caught my eye, and I looked long and hard.

It was the whales again, clearly visible, their bodies shimmering, twitching, luminous—four or five of them moving back and forth slowly in front of the cove and the net. And behind the twine, the fish were stirring again, where before they had been quiet, the water dark.

They seemed to be waiting for something, the fish and the whales both. That was the strange part. But I was cold and tired, and after a while I went back to the pilothouse and slept.

I woke early to lie in the bunk, half awake, trying to remember what it was that seemed so unusual. Then I sat up suddenly; it was the silence.

Before there had been gulls and cormorants around the net all the time, diving and crying, fishing for the herring. But that morning, there was only a hushed stillness.

Jim was already up, in the outboard, crisscrossing the cove with the sounder on.

He found nothing. The fish were gone.

And to the west, under a threatening sky, stark white against the gray, were four white sardine carriers, all bound for Seal Island.

A somber and silent crowd packed up boxes and tents. The lobsterboats disappeared back toward Vinalhaven.

Finally there was only Jim's gang and us, and Peter's son who stayed to help get the twine back, the fourth generation of that family to fish herring on Seal Island.

A light rain began to fall; the men began the tedious job of hauling the net back into the dories, flaking it down for easy setting out again.

Exactly in the middle of the net was the hole. You could have driven a truck through it. The torn piece hung limp. Without ever stopping in the rhythm of hauling, Jim took up the slack, pulled that section clear, and hung it over the side of the dory for patching in town.

It could have been a whale, or maybe just the tremendous weight of the fish finally rending the twine. There was no way to tell what had really happened.

"Oh, we had 'em, Dad, we *had* 'em." With little success, Tim, Peter's boy, fought back the tears.

"Nope." Peter looked at the dory, half full of twine now as the men worked their way across the cove in an unbroken rhythm. "You never have 'em until they're in the carrier, headed up the bay. . . ."

Nine

I woke to the thinnest light in the eastern sky, the pilothouse sticky, oppressive. Half asleep, I dragged my pillow out on deck and fell back asleep at once.

Images of the night before, half remembered, floated through my mind: a night of seiners steaming up and down the bay, followed by the carriers from island to island, looking for fish and finding none, one by one giving it up until there were just two carriers left, and David, who hadn't said a word all evening.

And at three a.m., five miles from the nearest land, he set and loaded us all.

David looked five years older than when I had last seen him: he had been lobstering all day and fishing herring all night, and it was telling on him.

Then we steamed east, bound through the islands to a lobster co-op some four hours away. But it came on foggy, and the dance between radar, compass, and chart in those unfamiliar waters was too much. Exhausted, I picked a little nook on the shore, slid in, dropped the anchor quietly, and collapsed into my bunk and dreamt.

In my dream, we lay in a lovely, still harbor. Amaretto was spotless, and on all sides were other boats—workboats, yachts, all lined up to buy from us. It was not herring we were selling, though, but vegetables. Both holds were full of boxed lettuce, tomatoes, peppers, cauliflower, broccoli, all fresh from our own garden on a field above the water. The crop, the boat, the holds were all sweet smelling, the people eager to buy from us. It was a good business. We made a trip every week, tending the garden in between.

There was no night work. We never saw herring one.

A voice interrupted my pleasant dream: "Hey, wake up, it's late. . . ."

"Uhhhh. . . ." I didn't want to give up the dream. I struggled not to lose it. A foot nudged me in the side.

"Hey, c'mon, we got five hundred bush to peddle, and it looks like a hot one. . . ."

I rolled over, pulled myself up into a sitting position, rubbed my eyes, smelled herring, blinked in the sunlight, remembered where we were and what we were doing. . . .

The hot weather came to lie on the coast, and the lobsters at last began to "crawl."

Many of the men began averaging a pound or more per pot per day—very good fishing. It meant that each day a lobster crawled into each of the tens of thousands of pots surrounding the island. Of course, not every one was a "keeper" of legal size, but still, the bottom must have been crawling with the odd, spiny creatures.

105

And for us, selling most of the bait to catch those lobsters, it meant that the days blurred into one another, a daze of unloading herring all day up and down the bay in a half dozen different places, washing down, fueling up, getting a quick bite, and sliding back down the bay at dark for another load from whomever we could get it.

Vignettes:

Afternoon, the harbor: from somewhere a curious sound, like live music, and we look up from our unloading but fail to find the source. Then the ferry steams around the corner with the entire high school band up on the bow, coming back from a trip somewhere.

Afternoon, the harbor: we have a hundred bush left, and we want to sell it, to wash the hold before we go out again. So we walk around, cajoling the lobsterboats in from hauling: "Hey, special price for you boys, ten bush for the price of five." And the lobstermen smile, warm up to the routine, and in an hour we are empty.

Afternoon, the harbor: we finish unloading on a hot afternoon, and as the lobster buyer, "Westside Jack," Ann, and I share a lobster sandwich and a beer, his grandfather comes in from hauling. He has a sixteen-foot wooden outboard and hauls his pots by hand; eighty-two years old he is, and spry as a twenty-year old. He sees one of his lobster pot buoys trailing behind our stern, cut off by our propeller.

"Hey," he cries out, "that's my trap you cut off." His face takes on a sly look. "So let's have eight bushels of bait, and we'll call it good." We give him the last eight bushels in our hold, and I am left with the lingering feeling that we'd been had.

Afternoon, the harbor: we lie at the fuel dock, fueling and watering up on a warm, late afternoon before heading out again. And above us, sitting on a bench in the sun, are a few old duffers, retired fishermen, sharing a beer, cackling to each other, pointing down at Amaretto, smiling, remembering.

Afternoon, the harbor: Amaretto and two big company carriers, all coming in at once, make their turns in unison, sliding into the wharf, the company carriers lying one on either side of us.

"A thorn between two roses," the other skippers call out to each other, and smile.

Early evening, the harbor, this one to be savored, happening once or twice a week: Amaretto and maybe a couple of other carriers all lying side by side at the wharf, with David or Jim or one of the other herring seiners tied alongside. And all of us jammed into one of the fo'c's'les, sharing stories and a couple of good, warm rum and Cokes before we slide down the bay. Finally someone gets to his feet. "C'mon boys, it's time." And the lines are quickly off, and one by one we slide out and through the moored lobster fleet, bound down the bay for another chase after the "wily kipper."

The 16th of August came with a curious smoky haze around the harbor. I smelled it from my bunk in the pilothouse, but looking out, saw only the lobstermen rowing out to their boats in the dim four-thirty light. Buying bait, each of them commented on it, looking around, wondering where it was coming from, what it was.

Finally, in the coffee shop, one of David's crew told us: "Seal Island's burning. We saw it last night, little flickers along the shore. We thought it was campers. There was a skiff there."

All day unloading our bait in that smoky haze that obscured the island, I wondered about the fire, about how bad it was. I wondered most of all about the birds, for the island was always alive with them, wondered if they still had chicks that couldn't fly, or if the young were grown and gone.

We stayed in that night; our markets were full. Ann went up to Tom's house and I stayed on the boat, listening to the radio. And David came on:

"Henry, can you see us? We're over here in this smoke. I got one out, but it's getting pretty thick. . . ." In the background I could plainly hear men coughing, choking. "I'm not sure how long we can stay here. . . ."

"Yeah, we're in the clear out here, David. I can see part of your mast through the smoke. It looks pretty thick in there."

A long while passed. No one said anything.

"You guys all right, David?" Henry's voice was anxious.

". . . Yeah, the wind's shifted now. C'mon in quick as you can and let's get these fish out. We were getting red cinders on deck there for a while."

The next day the haze lifted, and we could see Seal Island at last. There was a big pall of smoke over it, drifting slowly away to the south, dominating the sky, the whole southern horizon. In the afternoon, volunteer gangs from the Hurricane Island Outward Bound School went out to try and put it out. But just a

"Hey, special price for you boys, ten bush for the price of five."

few hours after they landed, an unexploded bomb or shell went off with a dull thud, and everyone evacuated. The fire was left to burn itself out.

The next day and the one after came cloudless and hot, and the fires burned unchecked. Now and again, we would stop whatever we were doing and look down the bay as another distant "whump" came across the water to us.

Seal Island: night, fog, smoke. We were in close, waiting for David to set, and through the fog and the smoke could clearly be seen the eerie orange glows of the fires, burning in seven or eight places at once, in the bushes, seemingly in the ground itself. The birds were wild, swooping angrily all around the boats, at us, as they never had before, and then back over the fires, in and out of the smoke. For all we knew, their nests were destroyed, their young killed. And we could do nothing. Just being in so close made us nervous about the bombs and shells.

"Amaretto, come on."

David was hard against the shore, set on the smooth bottom. The fire was very close, his boat, the rigging, silhouetted against the flames and orange smoke.

"Quick as you can now, we're getting a lot of smoke here. . . ."

We slid in gingerly. On David and his crew's faces, concerned, smudged looks. Hot ashes sifted down on us. They took our lines quickly, tied off the corkline on our rail, and had us brailing faster than ever before. Now and again the wind would shift, sweeping the hot gassy smoke down on us, and we'd stop, turn away, choking, trying to hold our breaths, hoping it would pass.

Finally we were done. "Let's get *out* of here," Ann yelled from the winch. Cornwallis huddled in the door of the pilothouse, looking out at the strange scene, probably wishing that he had stayed in town. And then the lines were off and both of us were running full bore, getting away from the island, the smoke, the fires.

"The birds," Ann said sadly, as we steamed north for Vinalhaven, for home. "The poor birds. . ."

And deep in the night, asleep in my bunk, twice I woke up to that odd hollow "whump" of long-hidden shells exploding from the heat.

In the evening, once again, we steamed just off the western tip of Seal Island to lie in smoke and haze, waiting for David to get a set of fish for us. And once, as we idled along, waiting for him to call us, I saw something on my radar screen just for an instant, and then it was gone. So I stopped, took the engine out of gear, and went up on the bow and looked. There was a long oily swell, and the light was very poor. But then, just for a moment, the sea fell away, and maybe fifty feet off our bow revealed a jagged wall of dripping rock, black against a black sea, barely seen at all, and as quickly covered up again in the swell. It was Malcolm's Ledge, an evil, unmarked reef jutting up suddenly from the deep water. We had drifted off the west'ard more rapidly than I had thought and had almost steamed over it.

Then David set, and we were in and brailing, with the glows of the fires still burning and the anguished cries of the birds clearly heard.

And that place that I had enjoyed so much before gave me a strange, uneasy feeling—the cry of the birds, the glow of the flames, and seeing Malcolm's Ledge appear so suddenly out of the black ocean—and I was glad when we were done and steaming up the bay for home.

Finally, a week after the fire started, we had an all-day, all-night soaking rain, and the fire was out.

The next evening we waited off the island in our usual spot for David, watching him, a dim shape in the night and the mist. He was in Sou'west Cove, and the fish were in shallow water up at the very head, too shallow to set the net.

As we watched, we could see the silent shadow that was David slide into the back of the cove, herding the fish slowly out as a cowboy might herd a bunch of skittish heifers, not crowding them, just easing them out until they were where he wanted them, and quietly, precisely, setting his net around them, or as much net as he could get out in that constricted spot.

He called us in, but I hesitated. The shore seemed right next to his boat, and there seemed to be little room for us.

"Aw, c'mon in, it's deeper than it looks."

"... down the bay for another chase after the 'wily kipper.'"

Cautiously, I eased in, Ann up on the bow, shaking her head, the shore a few feet away. Only the rising tide gave me courage. If we grounded, we would soon float free.

From where we brailed the fish out of David's net, I could have jumped ashore from the bow of the boat. We were in a little pool of water with steep rock shore on three sides. He had set the net in there like a hand into a glove.

But the silence, the smells, were oppressive. Always before, around the island had been the constant cries of gulls and storm petrels, birds that sought the wildest, remotest spots for their nests. Now there was only the slow wash of the sea against the rocks outside, and a faint, burnt, dead smell.

"It was kids. . . ." David nodded over toward the island.

"How do you know?"

"There was a skiff there that first night we saw the fires. Even then it was burning in six or seven places. It wasn't an accident." He nodded over to his crew. "Some of the boys recognized the skiff. . . . It was kids."

"But why?"

"Meanness, something to do, who knows?" He shrugged again. "Pity, though. . . . They could have done something else for their kicks." He waved to the men, the lines were untied, and they disappeared into the black.

And Seal Island one more time, a few days later, called over by an unfamiliar boat whose chain-smoking skipper sold us some 20,000 pounds, all they had for the night and too few to run to Portland with. When we were done and cleaned up, one of his crew came over to visit for a while.

He said they had spent many nights looking for fish, steaming from Gloucester north, the skipper at the wheel for twenty, thirty hours at a time, chain-smoking Camels, the sonar on, constantly looking. Once, he said, he had come into the wheelhouse to find the skipper grimmacing in pain and holding his chest. He asked him if there was anything wrong.

"Oh, no," he said, gritting his teeth against the pain, "it's just one of those heart attacks. They're painful, but you 'kin get used to 'em."

And as we loaded, I looked around the island, seen for the first time in daylight since the fire.

Of the graceful island that I remembered, with grasses and bushes and wildflowers, there was nothing. It was brown, dead, scarred, silent, the water along the shore discolored from the mud and the ash. It could have been Atka, or Attu, one of a thousand bleak rocky islets stretching across the Bering Sea between Alaska and Russia. But even they had flowers, birdlife in the short summer.

On Seal Island there was nothing. It was silent, dead.

Ten

September 1: a west wind in the night, red leaves in the morning, the day seeming to cry, "Summer's gone, winter's coming." The change made me worry about the weeks and months ahead, for we still hadn't made a season.

Then darkness, with David, around every island in the southern bay, the wind making up stronger and stronger. I didn't think it would be a "chance." Then, finally, after midnight, the call:

"There's a bunch here by the rock if you want to come over. . . ."

So we slid out from behind the lee of No Man's Land and headed for Matinicus Rock—a lonely outpost, a stark few acres of granite topped with a white lighthouse, the last bit of land before Spain, England, and Africa. I didn't see any shelter from the wind and the sea when we first got there, didn't see how we would be able to load even if David got a set. But then, when I got a little closer, I saw that he had found a lee, the smallest sliver of calm water to work in, a few acres at most.

"Ah . . . you may as well go up and put a line on that buoy. It might be a long wait."

So I did, shut the engine down, and slept deeply, with only the rush of the seas on the windward side of the island for noise.

"Have a look out back." Ann's hand was on my shoulder.

I pulled on a sweatshirt against the cold and went out behind the pilothouse to a dramatic scene: the night, very black, the sky clouded over thick, the moon not yet up. Then the great beam of the light swept over our heads and shone on David's boat, just for an instant. I saw David, intent at the wheel, his crew like statues on the stern, ready to set the net at a moment's notice.

Then I saw the school of fish, the same glowing cloud that I had seen before at Seal Island, the water firing brilliantly—it was a duel, just David and his men, and a wary school of herring, each group feinting, circling the other.

"Amaretto."

"Right here."

"Say . . . how 'bout cutting loose and letting the tide carry you clear, but don't start up until you get out a ways. These fish are awful jumpy . . . and they're the only ones I've seen all night. . . ."

When I went forward and untied, the underbody of the buoy and the mooring chain were glowing in the night, lit up by the fire in the water. I let the tide carry us a couple hundred yards down the shore before we started up, and when we did, bright arrows darted from beneath us in all directions—mackerel, started by the noise.

David moved up the beach a little, got beneath the sweep of the light, and became a glowing wake in the darkness. When he turned, sometimes I could see the sonar and radar screens, the glow of someone's cigarette from the stern. But

112

he hardly needed electronics with the fish, the bottom, lit up in that dim and eerie night.

"Ohhh . . . these fish are wicked nervous tonight. There's just the littlest patch of soft bottom here where I can set . . . and that moon'll be up soon. . . ."

I looked to the east. There was a faint light behind the clouds. The moon was coming. A long while passed. We jogged just inside where the lee began, and finally I dropped the anchor and went out behind the pilothouse to look.

David would swing in toward the shore, uptide of the fish, make a circle, and try to force them a little closer to the patch of smooth bottom, herding the herring as I'd seen him do before. But the more he pushed them the jumpier they got, the glow pulsing more, flickering brightly in the black water.

I looked up. The clouds were beginning to break up, and I could see stars in a few places, but the moon was still hidden. He would have to get them before the moon got much higher, for the pale light of a good moon would drive them mad.

On the stern of his boat a tiny light winked on: the end light of his net. He was getting ready to set. He made one last swing uptide to herd the fish closer, over the sand. But the fish resisted, as if they sensed the sand, the smooth bottom, the waiting net, and they moved but a few dozen yards. The wake circled uptide one more time. This was the moment; I sensed it.

All at once the glowing school of fish pulsed once brightly, broke apart into thousands of little specks in the water, and fled back up the shore a hundred yards to knit together again, glowing, quivering over the rocky hard bottom.

"Shit." The radio spoke; the net light winked out. David swung the boat up the island shore, got uptide of the patch of dim light in the water, and the whole process began again. An hour passed, slowly, David herding the fish down the shore, a tedious job, the fish even jumpier now. The sky was growing lighter, more stars appeared in the rifts in the clouds, time was short. Closer and closer he herded them to that invisible patch of sand. The end light of the net winked on in the stern again. I looked up. The edges of the clouds were tinged with yellow, and the moon was coming fast; it was then or never.

The school of fish drifted out over the sand, the net light dropped into the black water, the corks and the leads clearly visible, a glowing curtain sinking into the water behind the boat in a graceful curve, starting around the fish.

"29. . .28. . .27. . .26. . ." A voice counted each ring along the bottom of the net as it thunked over the side. When the count reached zero, the circle would be closed, the fish trapped.

Ann touched my arm. I looked up. A great rift had opened up in the sky, and the moon's light flooded out over the water a mile west of us.

"16. . .15. . .14. . .13. . ." The circle was half made, the school of fish clearly visible, glowing in the half circle of net. But they sensed the net, and began to move away from it toward the open water. David speeded up a little.

"9. . .8. . .7. . .6. . ." The gap was closing. Fifteen seconds and it would be done.

The moon broke clear of the clouds. The sea was a shining plain, transformed in an instant. By David's bow, in the narrow gap of open water between net and boat, there was a flurry in the water and the fish were gone.

We lay side by side. David's men pulled in the last of the net. No paper cups tonight, just the bottle. I took a pull and handed it back to David. He knocked back the last inch in a long pull. Carefully, holding the bottle in two fingers, he dropped it between the boats.

"Let's go home," he said.

Summer made its last stand: we swam in the quarry. There were children playing, lying on the rocks. The air, the sun were hot.

Then a night came stormy with violent squalls, wind, and thunder. Amaretto lay anchored between rocky islands with little room to swing; the squalls shook the boat, while we kept watch anxiously.

The morning came clear, the sky washed clean, the air from the north crisp and cool. Summer into fall again, overnight. Along the shore, the men spoke of the "fall spurt," when the lobsters make their move away from shore, off into the deeps. And the men move their gear out farther and farther, down the bay.

An early September evening: Amaretto and us, two miles south of Seal Island, David off to the south'ard, steaming, looking. In the afternoon the plane had spotted a good bunch of fish, but by the time we arrived, the "Gloucester boys" had appeared out of nowhere, six or seven large steel boats, great noisy pools of light in the darkness. They had giant nets, half a mile long and two hundred and fifty feet deep, and they could pump millions of pounds of fish aboard.

It was a sickening sight, for the great deep nets broke the fish up, driving what was left too deep for David's smaller, shallower net. Only after seven hours' steaming did he find something to set on, far from the harbor, all lights and land over the horizon, out of sight, and he called us in to load.

He had been going hard for most of the summer by then. Even on nights that he had no market, no one to buy his herring, he'd often be out cruising around, just seeing what the fish were doing. When he came aboard at last, his face was puffy, his eyes dead. We shared one drink, started on another, and he nodded over at his boat, his men.

"Used to be this was all you needed."

Dawn wasn't far away, and counting the last two nights out fishing, I figured this was his third without any real sleep.

"Made a good living at it, too."

He had a Cadillac parked over on the mainland, and in more prosperous times he'd take his crew or friends down to the games in Boston—the Celtics or the Sox. But for most of this year the car had sat disused, idle.

"Used to be, the end of a season, a guy'd have something."

David had aged noticeably even in the short time that I had known him, running on strength, on youth, never really stopping.

"When you had a body of fish in here like that, you could work on 'em for a while, weeks sometimes, when it was just us little boats."

His shoulders, his whole body drooped with exhaustion. We took another pull at the bottle, and he jerked his head over to the west.

114

"You saw it. Four hours those guys were out there, and then we couldn't hardly catch a fish. Those schools were all broke up."

His crew was done, waiting for the lines to be off and they could hit the sack.

"It's gonna' be the end to it. Those big boats'll pooch it for us all. You watch. . . ." Then he was gone, and Annie and I were cleaning up the boat, getting ready for the long steam back.

And when we were done at last, and she went below to sleep, and the lights were off and we were steaming, I looked out and there were only stars and the Big Dipper over the bow, guiding us home, twinkling as they never did in the soft summer air. Fall had snuck up on us without my ever really thinking about what was ahead. It hadn't been much of a season for anybody that year—when there were fish around, the market seemed always to be for something else—for big ones when there were only small fish to be had, for sixes when the islanders had fives. As we followed the bobbing, faint light a couple miles ahead of us that was David, I thought about him and what he had said.

The talk about the "net that pooched the North Sea" kept coming back to me.

There was a tradition with the local boats, and it was this: when someone had a big set and filled his "market," he gave what was left in the net to whomever else was around. That way the fish, often dead by then, weren't wasted, and everyone got a share. Nothing was asked except that the favor be returned if the situation was reversed.

But a couple of times when the big outside boats, the "Gloucester boys," had been around with their big nets, driving the fish deep so that the local boats couldn't get any, they would have maybe half a million pounds in a set and only be able to load, say, half that into their holds. But instead of offering what was left to the remaining fleet, they'd just open their net, and the dead fish would sink to the bottom, wasted, hundreds of thousands of pounds at a whack.

We had a day of unloading, a day of wind, then a peach of an Indian summer day with a breeze from the west and more leaves in the streets and the harbor. Of fifty lobsterboats, only fifty punts and skiffs remained. Every single man was after the lobster.

In the evening, an acquaintance and his ladyfriend, visiting the island, stopped down to the boat. Might they go out with us? They brought wine, and we slid out between the reefs, down the bay, drinking wine and talking as the sky colored and darkened before us.

And in a single short hour came a transition that subdued us all. From dusk in a quiet harbor surrounded by gingerbread houses and bright elms and maples, the first stars found us in the lee of a little dot of an island, a few acres at most, low, treeless. There was a cabin, and a skiff on the shore, but no smoke or sign of life to be seen. The lights on the distant mainland shore twinkled, cold and distant, and David was a shadow, a wraith, flitting along the shore, looking for his fish. Our friends stared in amazement at it all.

The reefs showed dull white, breaking in the darkness, but David moved unerringly, twisting his boat around the ledges until he found a bunch, worked

115

them, herded them away from the rocks and out into the deeper water, the smoother bottom. For our guests it was new, and we explained it to them, and after a while they sensed the drama, what it was that he was doing with no lights. Then just for a moment, because the stars were bright, they could see the dim glow that was the fish, and they understood.

The little light dropped off the stern into the black, the voice called out the numbers, the corks circled behind the boat, and it was done. David's decklights suddenly went on and he called us in. I brought the boats together, made the lines fast, and it was the same scene again at the end—the four figures in oilskins all staring down at the water, working the net up, then finally, after fifteen minutes of hard pulling, the fish breaking the surface, boiling and flipping, filling the air with the noise and their bright bodies—as always, a powerful, unexpected sight.

"Look." Ann saw it first, and put the spotlight on it—the very eastern point of the island close at hand, the tide sweeping us down on it. The short sea broke against the rocks, the barnacles, and the seaweed, all sharply etched in the beam of the light.

There was nothing that could be easily or quickly done. The boats were tied together, the net between us was full of fish, and the tide was sweeping us on. Whatever was to happen would do so quickly. David stepped aboard, and we walked up to the bow together, watching the point grow closer and closer. For a moment it seemed impossible that we not be swept ashore, but then the tidal current rebounded, carrying us with it, and pushed us around the point and into the deeper water beyond.

We took all that was in the net; it almost filled us. David wanted to set again, but before he could, the north wind came up strong and quick, and in just five minutes we knew it was time to head for the corral. In the lee of that unseen island, sand and dirt whirled down on us, and beyond it we could see the phosphorescent tops of the building seas.

David disappeared ahead of us, and for a lonely two hours we bucked up into the lee of the land. The windows of the pilothouse ran with water, and every fifteen or twenty minutes I'd see the ghostly glow of a big one breaking ahead. I'd chop the throttle, and Amaretto would slow just enough to avoid burying herself completely. But still there would be green water running back on both sides of the pilothouse, and once or twice, looking forward, it seemed as if the only things sticking out of the water were the mast and the pilothouse. Ann and I said nothing, as if it were what we were used to night after night. Our company was silent too, but where they gripped the windowsills of the pilothouse, their knuckles were white, their dimly seen faces, strained.

We made the land at last, sliding in under the beam of the tall lighthouse on Heron Neck. The sea died away, and we rounded the point and entered the harbor. Our guests climbed the ladder to the wharf in the starry, breezy night and looked around them in amazement. When they said their good-byes, I sensed that they could hardly believe that two so different worlds could exist so close together—the harbor with the boats sailing back and forth on their moorings, and that wild, black, and malevolent world beyond.

116

Another night beneath a mackerel sky, a deck of thin, fish-shaped clouds: we set out across the western bay to follow Jim close under the mainland shore. Above us were houses, people in living rooms watching TV and sitting by cozy fires, while below we slinked along the beach, blacked out, showing no lights.

But the half moon rose unusually bright, playing in and out of the clouds and spooking the fish, breaking them up, and it was only deep in the night, long after moonset, that Jim was able to set and get what we wanted.

"It makes 'em crazy," Jim said, drinking a cup of coffee on deck as his men cleaned up the seiner. "This time of year it doesn't take much a'tall to spook 'em. . . . We've been watching another bunch in Crockett's River, hoping they'd come ashore and we'd have a crack at 'em, but now with this moon . . . I'm not sure we'd be able to hold 'em."

"You got market?" I asked, for in the fall, it didn't make much sense to stop fish off unless you had a ready market for them.

"Sure, plenty of market for stop seine fish," Jim said. "It's just these that they don't want." He nodded down at the fish in my hold, perfect, uniformly sized fish, but too big for sardines. "Not unless there's nothing else around."

Two mornings later Ann and I sat in the coffee shop, chilled to the bone, up all night getting a load of fish a few at a time, and unloading them since five in the morning. Tom was there, excited, telling what they had seen the night before.

"Perfect fives," he said, looking around the room at the other men from his gang, all tired and ragged looking from another long night in the skiffs, cold and wet, waiting for the fish to move in. "Just sitting there on that hard bottom where you can't touch them."

"You gonna get 'em?"

"Dunno. They're movin', and real itchy they are . . . so late and the water cooling off fast, the moon coming on and all. They might stick around, or they might take right off . . . but they're just what the cannery wants now—just the right size, and a big bunch, bigger even than that one at Seal Island. God only knows what would happen if we were ever to get the twine around them. . . ."

Another spit of rain rattled against the glass. Ann and I stood up. We still had most of a trip to unload, a bushel at a time around the harbor, and we weren't looking forward to it very much.

That night, while we worked the outer islands with David, tracking a school that he finally got just before dawn, Jim and his men waited in the fog. And in a shallow little inlet that hadn't seen fish in years, the last place anyone would have figured for a big shut-off, the fish came ashore.

The early part of the evening had come with thin fog hanging along the shore, a sort of sea mist more than anything else. The plane couldn't fly in it, and Jim had put his crew into three skiffs, each with depth sounder and radio, looking in all the coves along the south shore. The big school had disappeared, and they were determined to find it again. At first no one could find anything, and they thought the fish might have taken off south, left the island for the winter.

Just by chance, Alton stumbled across them.

"It was the *big* one, the one you always talk about getting," he said. The waitress brought another round of coffees. Outside was the harbor, another blustery fall day.

"I couldn't believe it when I first went in—they went back into the river after all. I'd just decided to take a pass through there, and when I got in I thought the sounder had busted, shorted right out—it just showed solid right from the surface right down to the bottom, and that couldn't be right.

"So I got out the pole . . . you know, the old sounding pole, like they used to use. We still have one in the skiff. And God, the cove was right solid thick with fish. I tried it in four different places and it was the same. Then I put my hand down, and I could *feel* the fish rubbing against it."

Jim interrupted. "When you 'kin put 'yer hand in the water and *feel* 'em. . . ." He just shook his head.

"But it was silent, see, that was the strange part—a cove like that full of fish, you figure they'd be flipping up on top or something, but *nothing*, there was no noise. It was spooky.

"So I called Jim, and they came right over with the twine, and they all looked around and could see it was full of fish. But . . . like . . . we were almost afraid to shut it off. We had to talk it over. . . . There were so many we would have liked to cut them in half somehow . . . make them easier to handle, but the way the cove was, you had to take 'em all."

Jim spoke: "I been herrin'in since I was six, starting out with my dad, and we never seen a bunch like that. Alton's right."

"But fish in a cove like that, so many pushed right together, you'd expect a commotion, a few flipping or something, some sort of show. But there was nothing."

"Oh, it was a bunch all right." Jim shook his head, just thinking about it.

"So we ran the twine, shut 'em off, and right away, the trouble started. . . . You could see they were jumpy . . . pushing against the twine . . . trying to get around the ends, pushing right up over the corks. . . . It was crazy. If those fish started to move, they'd just take the twine with 'em. No way could we hold 'em. . . . We started setting out pockets right away, to break the fish up into smaller bunches, and each time we'd rig a pocket, the fish'd pour right over the twine and fill it. Five pockets we set out, and filled each one quick, right full."

"There was fifty trips of fish there if there was one," one of the other men added. "It . . . would have made a winter. . . ."

"And we almost had 'em, we came that close. . . . Set all the pockets we had, busted ass to get 'em done. You could see the moon comin'. . . . Set all the anchors. . . ." Tom's voice trailed off, and he shrugged.

There was a long silence.

"It was the moon." Tom shook his head. "If it weren't for the moon, we could have held 'em."

"We were just getting the last pocket set. All the anchors were rigged. We just were beginning to think that maybe we had a chance at holding 'em after all . . . just for the night, and we'd get a bunch of carriers in there in the morning and

118

start takin' out, ease the pressure on the twine . . . maybe even get 'em all out, since the fact'ries are hungry. . . ."

"Aagggggghh. . . . Then the edge of the goddamn moon came up over that hill on the side of the cove . . . and it was like those fish just went *wild*. All at once, the whole cove was a solid mass of boiling fish. They just went crazy . . . burst right through the twine, drove through some of the pockets, went over the corks in the others . . . drove *ashore*, almost a thousand bush drove *ashore* . . . they were that crazy."

"There's a few fish left in one of the pockets, and that's about it."

"C'mon, boys." Jim stood up. "We got to clean up that mess."

A scraping of chairs, a pulling on of coats. Tom turned to me for a moment on the way out. "You know, if we'd just sold one bushel in *ten* of what we shut off this year, it'd 'a been a season. . . ."

And in town, acquaintances, shopkeepers were subdued. Everyone knew of the herring the night before, of what might have been. In a small community, it would have gone a long way.

In the late afternoon we steamed to the west, to Metinic Island. The fog was thick. Finally I slowed the boat, took it out of gear, and peered ahead. A stony beach appeared, and a grassy field. I called out to Ann and we were anchored.

"It could have been the Hebrides, those wild and lost islands off Western Scotland."

119

It could have been the Hebrides, those wild and lost islands off Western Scotland. There were no men—only birds, and wild, long-haired sheep. We went ashore, and the fog swirled around us. The sheep kept their distance, dim shapes at the very limit of vision, wary, spooked by our presence. Amaretto disappeared behind us. We walked up a long slope. Shapes appeared out of the fog ahead—the peaked roof of a building laying on the grass, the walls perfectly collapsed beneath it. There was a house with the windows unbroken. Inside were a rusty stove and books on a shelf, but all disused, the calendar on the wall ten years old.

Trailed by the sheep, for two hours we walked around that lonely place, along sheep paths worn in the waist-high grass, past more forlorn and abandoned buildings, our world a circle of wet grass and fog.

Away to the west ten miles was the mainland. There would be lights, noise, cars in the streets. But on that island, all was silent, wet, still. The sense of man as intruder, interloper, was pervasive, and we were relieved finally to return to the skiff, see the boat loom out of the fog before us, listen to voices on the radio, eat dinner in the cozy fo'c's'le. When I went out on deck again after dinner, the fog had come in thicker, and of the island there was nothing. Even the beach was lost in swirling gray and the coming night, as if it had never been.

Once again I lay in the pilothouse bunk and slept, with the fog pouring in the open windows, filling the room. After midnight, I heard my name on the radio; it was David, and we hauled in the anchor and got underway, all vision stopping at the windows, the world but green images shimmering in a little box bolted to the wall. Threading a needle, we crept with rocks and ledges close, waiting on all sides, until finally we made the deep water beyond.

It was a huge set he had, in a place where other boats had crisscrossed, looking for fish and finding none. Again, we plugged Amaretto, taking all we could carry, and barely made a dent in the living mass of fish beneath the boats. Another carrier appeared out of the fog and took a load after us, and then David's men let the end of the net go, and enough fish to fill two or three more boats swam off silently into the night.

We steamed up the bay for home, through the outer ledges and in the back door to the harbor in thickest fog.

As always, on such a night, I was wound up and tense from feeling my way back in the fog, so I was glad to meet Corn on the wharf, to walk. I would leave him on Vinalhaven when we went out those fall evenings; he liked it better that way. With the window of my pickup open, he had a dry place to retreat to. He spent the evenings with his dogger friends in town, yet always heard us when we made the harbor, and was there on the wharf when we slid in.

Images of the night hung before me: of the island that we had visited—so wild and lost. And of David. On a night when you could barely see the bow of the boat, in an area others had searched for a trip of fish, he happens upon a school, scratches 150,000 pounds off the top, and turns the rest loose. It was said he had powers, magic with the herring, and now I was sure of it.

120

Eleven

The equinox storm came right on time—a good three day southeast gale that drove into the harbor, chafing Amaretto against the pilings and her lines. Beyond the harbor the ocean was wild, driving white across the ledges, throwing solid spray into the trees on Green's Island.

I climbed up to the wharf, checked the lines on the pilings, and walked up to the inn. It was a tall-windowed, stately Victorian building sitting on a little rise overlooking the harbor. With two big woodstoves, it was the natural gathering place on a day when the bay was feather white and the rain slashed against the windows.

The boys were sitting around one of the woodstoves drinking something hot and rummy.

"They're still there. I think it's the same bunch." Tom slid his chair a little closer to the heat. Half a dozen other fishermen lounged around the dining room and the kitchen, talking or playing darts.

"What about this?" I asked, waving out the tall windows at the wild sea beyond the harbor. "You could hold 'em in this?"

"Naw, it's OK. . . . They're in the lee up there. But," he jerked his head around the room, "about every other gang on the whole island is up there too. . . ."

"Getting late, isn't it?" Ann said. All the herring gangs had started to bring in their dories from the coves around the island. We were surprised that they would still try for a shut-off with the weather as it was.

Tom nodded. "Yeah, this'll probably be the last shot we get. Be a skinny winter if we strike out again. . . ." He shook his head, took a long pull at his coffee. "Too skinny. . . . You know, all you really need is one good shut-off . . . just one good bunch of fish with the market right, and that's your season. Remember the boys in T-Harbor?"

I nodded. Everyone in the herring business knew about it. Tenant's Harbor was just twenty miles to the west. In July, an immense school of fish had been shut off there. The fish were just what the canneries wanted; the weather was perfect. For three weeks they loaded carriers, three and four and five a day, and their season was made.

"Just one shot like that and you got it made."

Another rain squall drove in from the south, rattling against the windows. Tom drained his coffee and looked out at the rain-blurred world. "But if you haven't made it by the first of October," he shrugged, "then probably you're not going to."

The rain let up at dark, but the wind didn't. It stayed strong, and a swell still drove into the harbor. The sea outside was fierce.

So we stayed in, slept late. In mid-morning we took Cornwallis in the outboard skiff around to the north end, where Jim's gang was trying for the "big one." The action was in the Thorofare, the channel between Vinalhaven and

"Beyond the harbor the ocean was wild."

North Haven. On both sides, in every little indentation and cove, were dories and lobsterboats, boats I had never even seen before, all anchored, waiting.

"Who *are* those guys?" We stopped at Jim's boat to ask about the unfamiliar fleet around the shore.

"Casco Bay fishermen," Jim said. "That's how hungry everyone is."

Casco Bay was fifty miles to the southwest.

We took Tom over to a line of Jim's dories. He and I began pumping out the rainwater with a couple of galvanized pumps.

"So where are the herring?" Ann called over to him.

"Over there." Tom waved off toward the middle of the channel.

"And where's your cove? How come your dories are out here?" All Jim's dories were anchored off a section of straight shore, with no hint of a cove where they could shut off fish.

"Ah. . . ." Tom stood up, both fists in the small of his back, giving himself a break from the pumping. "That's the rub."

"You mean all those guys from Casco Bay got coves and you guys haven't got any place to set? What happened to 'a dory in every cove?'"

Tom shrugged. "There's only so many dories. . . ."

He looked around, as if to see whether anyone was listening—a superfluous gesture, since no one was within a half mile of us.

"We might try a round haul."

"Huh?"

"Just make a big circle out here in the flats. . . . Anchor off the twine, like in a shut-off, but without a cove. Jim figures it's the only chance anyways. He says those fish won't even come ashore. . . ."

"How's the market?"

"God, the fact'ries are crying for fish. Those fish are on the hard bottom now, but they're getting real jumpy. It's that time of year. . . . They might be gone for good in a couple of days." He looked around the shore. Everything was red and yellow, and the tops of some of the trees had already lost their leaves. "The first good northerly, these fish'll be gone. . . ."

We finished pumping out the dories, dropped Tom off, and took one last look around before heading back to the harbor. In almost every cove were boats and men, the tension a tangible thing.

Dusk: too windy again to go out. I cleaned up the pilothouse and waited for the engine to finish charging the batteries. Outside in the mean cold light, boats moved in the swell. I noticed that David's boat wasn't on the mooring, and wondering where he'd be on such a night, I called him.

"David. . . ."

"Hullo . . ." he came back to me. In the background I could hear his engine idling, and the sound of his sonar, the fish finder.

"What's going on out there?" There was still a lot of wind and a hell of a swell, and I couldn't think he'd be able to load anyone on such a night unless he found fish in a lee.

"Ah, just sailing 'round and 'round."

"Where's Henry?"

"Oh, he's back to town. . . . I didn't b'lieve we'd be able to do much. . . . It's still quite . . . shitty out here. . . ." His voice trailed off.

"See anything?"

"Ohhhh . . ." a long pause, "there's a few little scattered bunches here and there . . . but it's getting quite . . . thinnnnn. . . ."

I wished him luck, shut off the engine, and climbed up the ladder, into the truck with just Cornwallis, for Ann had settled into the warm fo'c's'le with a book for the night. The harbor was dark then, and the wind seemed to be coming on again, raw and cold.

We drove around. In the beer store I ran into one of David's crew, a big, blond, soft-spoken man. I asked why he wasn't out with David.

"Oh, he's out alone . . . just looking around. . . . He does that a lot, even when he's got no market, just to see what the fish're doing. Didn't you ever know that?"

We steamed through the Thorofare two days later, and nothing had changed—along the shore, all the boats and all the men still waiting, "camping" on the fish.

Our course took us over the deep hole where the fish were, and I turned on the sounder and had a look at them—a dark, irregular shape on the white paper, hanging along the bottom of a little basin, but a thick mark; a good body of fish, winter's money for any gang that could get around them.

And how different the scene along those shores from just a few weeks before. Then there had been yachts on the moorings, people on the floats and on the lawns and in the houses along the shore. But now the moorings were empty, the floats drawn up on the shore, the houses boarded up, and in the sparkling fall sun, the land across the bay shimmered, mirage-like, as it never does in summer's soft air.

Tom was there, with Jim and the rest of the gang, staying aboard the seiner, there for the "duration"—until someone caught the herring or the fish left the bay, whichever came first.

"What's it look like?" I slid Amaretto alongside for a moment.

"Something's gonna have to happen soon," Jim said. I could feel the anxiety in his voice. "Sky's clear and glass's high." He feared the north wind that often comes after a westerly that time of year.

"Whose shore is this, anyway?" I wondered what the fisherman who "claimed" that shore would have to say.

"Todd Davis."

"And what's he think of all this off his shore?" I waved at his seiner, the five dories full of twine anchored behind.

"Ah, well, he's none too pleased about it." Jim smiled. "He came by and I told him right out what we wanted to do, and he laughed and said it couldn't be done." Jim looked out past the dories. "But if that bunch of fish moves out of the hole and across these flats, we'll have a crack at 'em all right, and then we'll see what he says."

We still had fish aboard when we got back to the harbor that evening, so we stayed in; the wind was keeping much of the lobster fleet in anyway. Ann and I sat in the coffee shop for a couple of crab rolls and fries, and then we took Corn and drove up to the north end of the island, along a dirt road through the woods, winding up to the top of a hill where I thought we might be able to see what was going on. Sure enough, we walked through the woods and found a little clearing on top where the hill fell away, revealing the wide channel below. We could see the twinkling lights of the mainland in the distance.

At first we could see nothing in the water, for the sky had clouded over, and the moon wasn't up yet. Then slowly our eyes grew accustomed to the dark, and we saw dim lights around the shores beneath us—boats and men waiting. Now and again there would be the flicker of a match as someone lit a smoke, or the phosphorescent trail of a seiner or an outboard boat moving around in one of the coves, looking for a sign that the fish were stirring, that this might be the night they had been waiting for.

The west wind was stiff and chill. Cornwallis snuggled up into a ball against it and went to sleep. But the channel below us was north and south, sheltered from its force.

We got cold and wanted to go, but just as we were about to get up I saw something out in the middle of the channel—the dimmest light in the water, shapes faintly seen, moving, like the schools of fish I had seen before. But it was fainter now, for the water was cooling, and the firing of the phosphorescence was less intense. So we pulled our coats tighter around us, found a place out of the wind, and sat again, wanting to see the outcome.

The dim glow in the water seemed to knit together as we watched, as if finally the fish had made up their mind to move. Slowly they started to slide off to the southwest, toward the deeper water offshore, the bay and the ocean beyond.

The flats, the smooth, shallow bottom where Jim waited, was right in their path.

Sounds, coming clearly across the water: an engine starting up, the thunk of an anchor hitting the side of a boat. I could just see Jim's seiner beginning to move, and flashlights weaving around on the line of dories behind. Then, clearly, the sound of voices, angry words. Another boat had come out from the shore to Jim's, and there was yelling back and forth. The words were indistinct, but the anger was unmistakable.

And then, finally, what everyone had been waiting for—the rattle of corks and leads, the long wall of a net being set over the stern of a dory. I strained my eyes, and could just see the dories towed slowly in a vast circle. Four dories full of twine they used to make that circle, almost half a mile of net. And behind the dories, a couple of outboard boats were working. Tom, I thought, and some of the others, setting anchors out as fast as they could to hold the great circle of net against the sweep of the tide.

It was the longest kind of shot. I watched in amazement as the net moved around the faintly shimmering body of fish, expecting at any moment to see the half-formed circle collapse upon itself in the current. But the men with the anchors were ready. They had planned it all out in advance, and they worked to set the anchors out almost as fast as the twine went into the water. For the moment, at least, the net seemed to hold.

The dim cloud of light that was the fish came to the edge of the net. Jim had set it right along their path, cutting them off from the deeper water they sought. The fish hesitated a moment, then turned and began working their way back along the net toward the dories, where the circle still had to be closed.

I heard the engine of the seiner speed up; Jim saw what the fish were doing and hurried to close the door.

And then it was done. The great circle was made. A faint sliver of moon came over the hill behind me, shimmering faintly on the water below, and the fish could no longer be seen.

"Think they'll hold them?" Ann asked.

"They'll be some lucky if they do," I said.

They had 'em, I was sure of that. Holding them would be something else again, in that uncertain spot with the moon coming on. But he had done it. They were behind the twine. I hadn't thought he'd be able to do even that. We climbed back down the hill, found the truck, and bounced along the potholed roads to the harbor with the heater on full.

Deep in the night, a new sound woke me. I pulled on a wool shirt and went out on deck. It was the wind, shifting from the west into the north, rattling the tin roof of the old fish plant, a poor sign for Jim and his gang.

By morning it was blowing like stink, north northeast, hardly a day for hauling. But a half dozen boats came by anyway, to bait up and be ready for it when the weather did break. The last was Rowie Martin, a shy, husky man from one of the other harbors around the island. He had been up there on the north end too, with a couple of dories, looking for a piece of the action. So I loaded him eight bush for the price of six and asked him how he'd made out.

"Didn't." He cleaned a thick thumbnail with a penknife. "Brought m'duries home thi'smarning."

"How 'bout Jim and his gang, how'd they make out?"

He looked across the harbor at the whitecaps outside, the thin, scudding clouds.

"Hanging on, I guess. . . ."

"Think they'll be able to get any out today?" If the market was as strong as Jim had said, they'd have boats lined up waiting for their fish.

Rowie shrugged, and pulled in his tie-up line. "Pretty hard chance up there 'fer the boys. . . ." And then he was gone, back around the corner to his own harbor, to fill his bait bags with our herring and wait for a chance to haul his lobster pots.

We took the table by the woodstove in the inn when we finished unloading our fish, and got good and warm for the first time since getting up that morning. As I looked out the window at the harbor, someone towed a string of dories in, probably from the north end, and after a while a few more men trickled in for a mug-up and to stand by the stove. They told me Jim had seven carriers anchored and waiting, with one "on the twine" loading when they left, but with the wind and no lee, it was a tricky chance at best.

But all afternoon passed, and still they didn't show up at the harbor, so I took that as a good sign, that they were still loading boats.

The wind seemed as if it might let go that night and let us sneak out for a chance at a trip of fish, maybe the last one of the season, the way things were going. So I hung around the harbor and the boat, waiting to see if it would be a chance, instead of driving up to the north end to see what was happening with Jim and Tom. But the wind still blew, clawing at the trees and working the boats up and down against the pilings. Finally, after midnight, I turned off the radio and drifted off to sleep.

I slept in that next windy morning. When I woke, there were Jim's seiner and all the dories, back in the harbor. I tracked them down finally, his whole gang, working in the parking lot, in insulated coveralls against the raw wind. They had a long piece of net stretched out. The hole they were mending must have been a hundred feet long.

Ann was there, helping Tom, holding the net as he sewed. I went over to them to ask what had happened.

"Could have done worse, I guess. We loaded four boats, and we had fish for a good dozen more." Tom's eyes looked dead. He and the rest of the gang looked as if they could use about a week's sleep.

He shook his head angrily. "Ah, Christ, we had the fifth boat on the twine, half loaded, and a wicked gust of wind came up. His anchor lines parted, and," he nodded at the long tear the men were working on, "that was the end of that. He carried right on through the net and took the whole ball of wax with him."

At dusk the wind let go at last. Ann and I chased David again, under a thin moon and across a confused, leftover sea, up the eastern bay, crisscrossing back and forth, waiting for him to find something to set on, watching him relentlessly tacking back and forth, his sonar scanning the cold waters. I would have given it up after five hours or so, especially since he had only us for market, but David never stopped. He quit the bay and sailed around the islands, through the ledges, while we waited in the deeper, safer water outside. Then finally south, away from the shore, out into the southern bay and finally the ocean, farther and farther out to sea, until the land lights disappeared over the horizon behind us, and finally he set.

"Take 'em all," he said, and we did, filling both holds, and the fish poured back out onto the deck, spilling into the ocean again to swim away, lucky, surprised.

The paper cups, the silent, waiting men, and then he was gone.

By the time we got the boat cleaned up and the hatch covers on, the moon had set, and there was only black ocean and dim stars—all land, all lights, even David, lost in it.

So from that nameless and lonely place we steered northeast, put the Big Dipper above the bow, and after an hour or so, the outer flasher, the lights of Vinalhaven came up over the horizon. In the blackest part of the night, we slid into the harbor, laid the boat against the wharf, and shut down the engine. The sudden stillness was overwhelming.

On the dock, my footprints were dark against the white frost. Ann put her hand on my arm for a moment when we were done tying up.

"Amazing, isn't it?"

"Huh?" I was beat, thinking of other things.

"This." She waved her hand at the boat, the wharf, the still fleet lying in the harbor, the blinking light marking the outer ledges, and then beyond: that black and silent place we had just returned from.

And I was struck again by the powerful mystery of the business we were in. Of David, steaming without a word for nine hours, farther and farther away from the land, and finally, in a place of only stars and sky and water, loading us in a single set of bright, surprised fish. Then of being alone out there after moonset, not a boat, or light, or land in sight, the old boat low in the water, her guards almost awash. And finally of putting the Big Dipper over the bow and steaming until the island came up over the horizon. Ann was right.

"Yeah," I agreed, "it really is."

Twelve

It was in the fall, when the fish were scarcer and the good nights fewer, that I got the best sense of David's true powers.

On the last night of September we waited on a lonely patch of ocean, three miles from land. A short distance away, David warily circled a target on his sonar, watching the clouds, the moon, waiting for his chance. The moon was large, the clouds moving, broken. Sometimes a thick patch would cover the moon, and the chase would intensify as David closed in. Then the clouds would pass, the moon would shine upon the water, and the fish would spook. David would back off and wait for the next time of darkness.

The ocean was cooler by then, the phosphorescence firing less brilliantly. I couldn't see the fish easily, as I sometimes could in the summer, but the contest between David and them was no less real for it. I could sense it as we lay to, rising and falling in the swell, waiting for him to set.

When at last he called us in, it was three in the morning. I had nodded off and woke up to the blackest kind of night, the moon down, and found them with a tremendous set, glowing visibly despite the reduced phosphorescence of the water. We took the corks and the men put their backs to the job of bringing the fish up, until the surface boiled with them, pushing the boats an easy fifteen feet apart, a solid ball of fish maybe fifty or sixty feet deep.

We loaded all we needed and more, both hatches full to the coamings and spilling out on deck, and of that great mass of fish, we had barely scraped the smallest number off the top. David waved to his men, they let the end of the net go, and we all watched as the huge body of fish swam off into the night.

"And next month the companies'll be crying 'fer fish, and there'll be none to be had . . ." David said bitterly. "Kind of a backwards business we're in."

If they could have sold them all as food fish, there would have been more money in that single school than there was in a whole month of fishing bait for us. But there was no market just then, only us taking those beautiful fish and selling them for lobster bait. The canneries didn't want them, for there were "shut-off" fish up and down the coast, and they could only handle so many a day.

He came over for a while, and we both watched the fish swimming out of the net. I noticed his hands for the first time, how white and shriveled they seemed, and I asked him about them.

"I haven't got any feeling left in them," he said, letting them drop to his sides. "Too many years in the cold water, I guess." He held up a booted foot. "Those guys aren't much better."

We made harbor in the dark. But along the shore, headlights were already moving, and dim figures could be seen on the floats, shoving skiffs into the water, men oaring out to their lobsterboats and readying for another long day before the really hard weather came. All our bait sold out that day. At dark we set

131

out again. It looked as if it would be a long night, so at 10:30 I gave it to Ann, told her the course, and lay down, exhausted.

Around midnight, Ann's startled voice woke me. I was out of the bunk and on deck in a moment. She pointed astern and to starboard. There, seen just for a single, awful moment, was a rock, a pinnacle, uncovered for a moment by the swell. Then it was gone.

I looked at my watch and realized I'd overslept and hadn't woken up for a course change. We had steamed full speed through a treacherous set of unlighted reefs, the Southern Triangles, and out into the deep water beyond. We were half loaded with fish. The rocks made up from deep water. If we had struck, it would have taken the bow and enough of the keel to open Amaretto up, and she would have slid off into the deeper water and sunk.

Ann brought me a cup of coffee, and we lay there for a few minutes, rolling back and forth in the swell, before I put it back in gear.

"Close one, eh?"

I nodded and then shook my head. "Look at us. We're so beat from hustling bait, I can't even keep awake any longer." I rubbed my eyes, looking down into

". . . have us deliver fifty or a hundred bushels to a spindly little wharf or shed somewhere, just at the top of the tide."

the radar. "Ah . . . you may as well get some sleep. I'm OK now. That won't happen again."

But instead of going down into the cozy fo'c's'le, she lay down behind me in the pilothouse bunk, and Cornwallis thumped down over in the corner by the door, and off through the night the three of us steamed, to fill the boat up again, get a few hours' sleep, and start shoveling it all out again in the morning.

Somewhere between midnight and dawn, on the edge of the ocean, David got us our fish, and we made it back to the harbor for a single sweet hour of sleep.

Then on a drizzly, mean, cold dawn, the first boats came alongside for bait. Ann worked the winch and I worked hip deep in cold, wet, dead herring for twelve long hours, broken only by moving the boat from one place to another around the harbor. The lobstercatchers sensed the end of the herring season coming now, and men we had seen only once or twice all summer stopped by to have us deliver fifty or a hundred bushels to a spindly little wharf or shed somewhere, just at the top of the tide.

The rain kept up, and there was no getting out of the oilskins or boots until finally it was full dark and the last of our night's herring were gone, salted down in big boxes and barrels, to be brought out later in the winter when there was nothing else around.

We went to Tom's house for hot showers, and he had dinner there for us. We started on the drinks and sat by the woodstove, just starting to savor the warmth of it, to unwind a bit.

But then David called, and said it might be a chance if we wanted to go. Though the body was weak, the spirit was willing, so we finished our dinners quickly, and stood up to go.

"So who needs friends if you've got money?" Tom chided us, but then he came along too, and in fifteen minutes we were headed down the bay in the black. The dark sea was restless; a wind was making up.

By Green Island David found them, in a narrow tide-swept gut between two little dots of land, stark, treeless, five miles from the next land. The tide was running hard, and there was only the smallest lee, but David, working without light and almost without noise, a shape only on the radar screen, nailed a good-sized school and called us in.

We could feel the wind beyond that little patch of shelter making up even harder, and the current was carrying us both out of the lee and into the nasty chop outside. I dropped over my light anchor—a seventy-five pound Danforth with a shot of chain and a long, heavy nylon line—hoping it would hold us there long enough to load. But it didn't; we quickly dragged off into the seaway, and there was no time to try again. With little said, we hustled to get loaded. We were soon out of the lee, and the boats worked heavily together, slamming into each other and squeezing the large fenders like thin balloons.

When we were full, Ann steered bow up into the wind and the sea, and Tom and I hauled in the anchor on the niggerhead of the winch, wondering what had happened, why it hadn't held. The piece of steel that came up at the end of the line was barely recognizable as an anchor—both flukes were twisted right back, the thick metal ripped like wet cardboard. The current, and the momentum of Amaretto with David's Starlight tied alongside, had probably fetched up the anchor hard, and it hadn't had a chance.

We jogged up into the lee of the land, as close under the shore as I dared, and then we ran out on deck to get everything squared away for the run back to Vinalhaven. When we were done, and the decklights were out, I picked our way between the two islands with the spotlight, for the land was low there, the tide high, and there wasn't enough of a target for the radar. On the eastern island was a cabin, little more than a two-room shack, and as I spotlighted our way through the narrow gut, the beam of the light played on the windows, reflecting back on us, an eerie sight framed on all sides by angry, whitecapped seas. Then we were in the clear again, and in the full force of the wind, bucking a short mean chop that drove spray like buckshot against the pilothouse windows.

The overheat alarm of the engine chose the middle of a squall to go off, and it was a frantic few minutes as I shut down and scrambled into the engine room to pull apart some plumbing and clean seaweed from the heat exchanger inlet.

It took only ten minutes to get going again, but David was on the radio after five, wondering why we had stopped. He was far ahead of us by then, up under the lee of the land and away from the wind and sea, but watching us on his radar all the same.

And when we made the harbor finally, at three o'clock in the blackest kind of night, I thought I saw David rowing ashore from his boat, and thought that he had sat there after dropping his crew on the wharf, listening to the radio, waiting to see our lights slide around the point, making sure that we were OK. It made me feel better for being out there when the wind came on and we were alone.

Deep in the night another gale swept in from the ocean. I woke, and outside the wind was a living thing, rattling the windows, banging something against the pilothouse, blowing leaves and dirt down onto the boat. I pulled on a sweater and went outside, and the wind clutched at me as I checked our lines and closed the banging engine room door. In the harbor, in the dim light, the boats tugged at their moorings. On shore a set of headlights moved around, shining out on the wind-ruffled harbor and the whitecaps beyond. But little swell made it that far in, and Amaretto only gently tugged against the pilings, and I was soon asleep.

In the morning we walked a road littered with leaves and branches, watching men in pickup trucks sitting and looking out at their dancing boats. Beyond the island that protected the mouth of the harbor, the ocean was angry, driving white across the ledges and reefs.

The storm blew into the next day, abating a bit in the afternoon. At dusk two big company carriers slid into the harbor on the off chance that the wind might let go, and they could get a trip of fish so the women in the canneries could have work in the morning. We went aboard to join many of the island herring fishermen, talking about the end of the season that suddenly seemed so close at hand. Then the wind let go, late, when no one expected it. It was almost midnight when there was a banging on the deck above, and we all put down the paper cups, climbed the ladder out of the fo'c's'le and stared around at the suddenly still evening. The wind had dropped right out, the boats in the harbor pointing all different directions.

So we all started up and headed down the bay, for the market was strong. David found a big school, and then all three seiners set as one, eager to get done and be off for home, for we were miles from the land, there was a big leftover swell, and the night was inky and ominously still.

And without even a warning puff, the wind came up out of the east. The first gust was an easy thirty-five. We were lucky: I had just come alongside David, but we were lying so that the wind blew us apart and him away from his net. I threw off the lines, and we were clear and away. But another boat got blown over his net, wrapping it up in his propeller, and had an uneasy tow up the bay for home.

That same first gust caught Jim aboard the carrier he was going to load, helping them to tie the net on, and the lines parted. A short sea made up almost instantly, and there was no way he could get back aboard his boat, so he had to ride the carrier back to the cannery on the mainland.

So on a night when we could have taken a whole trip and sold them quickly, an easy couple of grand in our pockets, instead we got nothing and fled up the bay for home, rolling the rails down in the mean sea. We made the harbor at four and were mighty glad to be in.

Dogfish Island, with its stone wharf and cozy lodge, is a comfortable berth, and on better nights we had lain there, sitting by the fire and sipping hot drinks, waiting for our call on the radio, buying fish the easy way. But on that October evening it was dark and deserted, the float drawn up into the woods. And instead of working the wide channel to the north, we worked the treacherous and unforgiving mass of ledges and reefs to the southwest.

It was an open place, exposed to the wind and the ocean, and it was a measure of our need that we found ourselves there. We idled along cautiously, checking every move before we made it, the strong tide ebbing and rocks breaking white on all sides. But a few thin fish hung there, and David worked back and forth, setting his net in a little basin barely larger than it was, the rocks close on all sides.

He'd call us in, and we'd slide alongside quick to brail out fifty or a hundred bushels before the current swept us down on the invisible reefs, and then it was throw off the lines, find a little lee, and jog while he searched for another set.

The way David and his crew fished those jagged bottoms was almost uncanny. It was bad enough just trying to keep eight feet of water beneath Amaretto, but when David set, his net was seventy or eighty feet deep. Yet he did so again and again in a place where momentary contact of the net with the bottom would mean several days' work putting it all together again. And all this with no lights on a dungeon-black night, in a body of water so strewn with islands and reefs above and below the surface that even the radar wasn't much good—there were simply too many targets too close together on the screen.

Finally, at four in the morning, we were loaded, but to get out we had to put our bow right on David's stern. We twisted and turned, following him, the targets around us merging in the center of the radar screen, and I could only breathe easy when at last we passed into the clear again.

Two nights later we went completely around Vinalhaven, following David. The sky was starless, inky, clouded over thick, our progress measured only by shapes sliding past on the radar and the lights of an occasional house, like a jewel hung in a black and featureless void. After five hours without a word, of scanning all the shores, in amongst the rockpiles, while I waited cautiously offshore, David called.

"The cupboard is bare. . . ."

"Not even a hambone?" I called back.

"Not even a dried-up cornflake. . . ."

The inshore fish were gone.

The next morning we spent in boatwork, the afternoon in picking apples. Then the night with David, far down the bay, following from island to island, the wind coming on, and finally the rain, too, in squalls, sweeping down on us, hissing across the water, rattling against the pilothouse.

Anyone else would have given up, but finally we dropped anchor under the lighthouse at Matinicus Rock while David found a school in amongst the rockpiles, herded them into the deep at last, and nailed them after two hours of patient work.

It was a small set, only half a trip for us, and he would have searched and set again, but the wind swung around even more, pooching what thin lee we had in the first place, so we called it good and headed up the bay. Another night we might have looked some more, but the season was late, and we were far from any good shelter.

When we were squared away and had set our course for home, I turned the wheel over to Ann and was immediately asleep in the bunk behind. But on such a night, in an old boat half loaded with fish, one sleeps uneasily, aware of the slightest change in motion or sound. So when the engine slowed, I was on my feet beside Ann, looking where she was pointing.

High up and off to port was a white light, moving fast. In my groggy state, I thought at first it was the masthead light of a large boat about to ram us, and I reversed hard. Only when we were stopped, rolling heavily in the swell, did I realize that it was a helicopter, hovering almost directly over us and sweeping us with its searchlight. We must have made an odd sight, an old sardine carrier stopped in the middle of the bay on a rainy, windy fall night, a number of heavy sacks of salt on deck.

David was far up the bay by then, probably just sitting in his boat waiting for us to make it into the harbor, and he would row ashore and be done.

Then I noticed something coming from the west, from the mainland, moving very fast: two lights, a red and a green, the running lights of a boat. As it got closer, I could make out now and again the gleam of a big bow wave. Thinking we might be called upon to assist some boat in trouble, I pulled on boots and a

136

sweater. But the newcomer stopped short of us and waited, just off our stern. And still on the radio, not a word.

"What happened?"

"That helicopter just appeared out of nowhere and put his light on us."

"And nobody called on the radio or anything?"

"Not a word." Ann looked worried.

"Well, hell, I'm not going to hang around here, rolling our guts out. . . . Let's go home." I put the boat in gear, pointing the bow toward Vinalhaven again.

"THIS IS THE U.S. COAST GUARD. DO NOT MOVE YOUR VESSEL." The overamplified voice rang in the night, and immediately behind us a blue flashing light appeared.

I took the engine out of gear and looked over at Ann, both of us uneasy. I called the Coast Guard cutter on the radio, but there was no response.

I tried again—no answer. The chopper and the cutter had every light trained on us, blinding us with the glare.

Finally I called the Coast Guard base on the mainland, some twenty miles away, and explained the situation to them.

"Yeah, listen, this is the Amaretto, and I'm about four miles from Vinalhaven, and you've got a chopper up here and a cutter on my stern, and they won't answer the radio and they won't let me go anywhere, so . . . what's the story?"

They said they had no boats in the area. Again I put it in gear, and from astern, the same angry metallic voice ordered us to stop. I called the mainland base once more.

"Yeah, this is the Amaretto again. I don't know what the poop is here, but you've got a chopper and a cutter right on top of me, and I'm getting real tired of rolling around. I'm heading into Vinalhaven. Pass the word."

There was no answer, but I knew that the chopper and the cutter were listening. The frequency was one they always monitored. I eased her into gear and gave her the throttle, and this time there was no blaring voice from astern, but the cutter positioned itself just off our stern quarter and the chopper stayed overhead. Both of them kept Amaretto bathed in light—the whole boat, but especially the foredeck. I thought it curious how the stack of brown eight-pound salt bags, twenty or thirty of them, seemed always to be the focus of the lights.

"Say, maybe I'll go up there and heave a few of those salt bags over the side, just for kicks. . . ."

Ann turned pale and dug her fingers into my arm. "Don't you even joke about it."

It had come to both of us at once—what the chopper pilot saw: an old sardine carrier with no fish pump. A young couple, the boat obviously loaded with something, and a bunch of heavy-looking brown sacks on the deck. It was pretty obvious they had us pegged for drug runners.

After a long hour, we slid between the ledges and into our usual berth at the wharf, and sure enough, before we had the lines on the pilings, the cutter slammed alongside for a no-fenders landing that had the paint chips flying off

137

poor Amaretto's side. A bunch of jumpy-looking young sailors with machine guns and drawn pistols leaped unsteadily aboard. One of them managed to blurt out that we were under arrest for suspicion of trafficking in controlled substances, or some such thing.

I wanted to make light of the situation, and give the skipper a bad time for his suave landing, but the sight of all those nervous nineteen- and twenty-year olds with their sweaty, twitching fingers on machine gun triggers made me nervous. They obviously thought they had a live one.

We put our hands up.

One poor soul was still wandering around our foredeck with a tie-up line from the cutter in hand, looking for something to tie to; he was used to cleats, probably, and we had only oak bitts.

"C'mon, you guys, what sort of horseshit is this? We got a load of herring, here. Look. . . ." Gingerly, for the guns were still drawn, I pulled one of the hatch covers back. The hold was full to the very top with freshly caught, sweet-smelling herring.

The officer in charge was a little taken aback. The guns went back into the holsters, except, I noticed, for one sailor's, who remained on the cutter, covering us all.

The officer pointed at the salt bags. "What are those?"

I pulled out my knife slowly, slashed the bag, and held out a handful of salt. He tasted it, then took out his own knife and slashed every bag, tasting a bit from each. Meanwhile the others had brought over a boathook and were poking it down into the herring, and beginning a rather thorough search of the boat.

Around the corner of the harbor came another cutter to lay beside the first, and another group of men came aboard to taste our salt and go through the whole interrogation. I heard the chopper land in the parking lot, and pretty soon two state troopers were climbing down the ladder to add their questions to the rest. More time passed. A *third* cutter came in to lie beside the other two, and there was yet *another* group of officials. They even brought David down, and he climbed down the ladder, holding his wrists up as if to say, "Put the cuffs on me."

The officials took turns marching up and down the ladder to use the phone on the dock, and the rain got thicker and harder. The whole business continued until dawn; we never got to sleep. Yet when they all left, there was never a word of apology for bothering us or for treating us so brusquely. And when all the cutters had gone, I looked around and noticed that although it was hardly a day "fer hauling," the harbor was full of men rowing out to their boats, casting off from their moorings, and coming over to us.

Not a single boat went out to haul that day, but in six hours we had all our bait sold, a record.

And almost to a man, they came alongside with a choice remark: "Well, I'll take a couple of bales," or, "C'mon, where'd ya stash it. We know what you're really doing!"

Later, in the street, when we had it all unloaded and walked up for breakfast, dog-tired, trucks would pull to a halt and men would call out, "Yeah, save me a pound," or such things.

But still I was haunted by the memory of that cutter slamming alongside us and those big-eyed kids jumping aboard with .45's and machine guns, fingers on the triggers, twitching all over and scared as hell.

What would have happened, I wondered, if, as David and I had discussed, we had steamed in and begun unloading the bait in the middle of the night, for the tide was right, and some of his crew wanted bait in their fish houses? What if the Coast Guard had been a little late, and, coming upon the scene of us unloading the boat at three in the morning into some little out-of-the-way shed, had decided to sneak up on us?

We worked with a tough crowd, and they wouldn't have taken kindly to being jumped in the middle of the night. Anything could have happened.

Thirteen

Tom's kitchen was cozy and warm; outside the wind swayed the trees around the harbor, keeping us in. There was a bottle of Scotch on the table, a dart board on the door. It was a better place to be than down the bay somewhere on such a night. The VHF radio was on top of the icebox; if anywhere around the bay or the island, someone called with a chance at some fish, we could be underway in a few minutes. But so far, the radio had been quiet.

We drank to the winter ahead, that it be a good one for all of us, but especially for Ann—she was off in the morning to nursing school. She had done a tremendous job on the boat, working without complaint or reward when things had looked truly bleak. The three of us had grown close.

"Henry . . ." David's voice came over the radio. Tom and I looked at each other. We hadn't thought anyone would be out on such a night.

A gust of wind slammed into the house, rattling the windows.

"Yisss . . ., David." It was the skipper on the carrier. In the background we could clearly hear the sound of his engine, rising and falling in pitch, as if the boat were bucking into a good head sea.

"Where . . . are . . . you?"

"Just coming out of town, just passing the breakwater now."

"What's it look like?"

"Ah . . . not very good. . . . We're not really out into it yet . . . but I don't believe we'd be able to do much business tonight, not unless we can find a good lee somewhere. . . . Whereabouts are you anyway?"

"Bull Cove . . ."

My dart arm stopped in mid throw. Bull Cove—it was an awful place, even in good weather. I looked over at Tom. "How'd you like to be down *there* tonight?"

He shook his head. He knew. That rocky hole would be whitewater, breaking on the ledges all the way across its mouth in tonight's wind, with maybe the tiniest lee way up at the head.

"Ahhhhh . . . that's no place for us tonight, is it?" the radio continued.

"Nooooo. . . . I thought it might be a . . . chaaaance, but it's quite . . . shitty . . ., really. . . . Pity though, there's fish here. . . . How's your courage?"

"Not good, David, least not for that place on this kind of night. . . ."

A seiner like David might be able to maneuver in there, knowing it the way he did and using his sonar, but for a carrier—an eighty-footer with the radar screen all cluttered with windblown spray, not being able to get any good targets, and no room for error . . .

David came back, "Well . . . I guess I'll have to find another bunch. . . . It's getting quite . . . rotten . . . in here anyway. . . ."

A rainsquall drove in over the island, blasting the side of the house like hail. Tom put another log in the woodstove, and we all sat down and ate. But our

141

thoughts were out there with David and his men, sliding in and out of the breakers, trying to find a handful of fish on that inky, terrible night.

"It's screwy," Ann said. "David's the best seiner around here. He could have loaded any number of boats, any summer night; the weather was perfect, and *now* the cannery decides they want his fish, and he's out there on a night like this. It's crazy. . . ." Her voice was angry.

"That's the herring biz," Tom said. "First your money, then your clothes. . . ."

I said goodbye and left them alone. My truck headlights picked out the whitecapped harbor, slashing rain, dancing boats. Somewhere close a radio was on; as I drifted off to sleep, I could hear voices: David and the carrier skipper.

In the windy, thin, first light, there was a bump alongside, and I looked out to see David's carrier coming alongside, empty. The night had been a bust.

Another evening: Amaretto and I, down the bay alone, helping Jim and Tom find the herring. We moved in great wide tacks with the sounder on; the search was frustrating and elusive. Where before, in summer, there were always scattered bunches of fish, faint smudges on the paper, too thin to set a net on, now the sounder was completely blank for long periods at a time—no feed, no fish, nothing but dark cold water.

But by No Man's Land, Jim found the fish, a little frightened bunch clinging to the hard bottom. Three times he set, scraping a few hundred bushels off the top. Each time, when I came alongside to load, Tom jumped up to help, and on the last set, when we were filled at last, he stayed aboard. We steamed off to the south, to find a mooring at Matinicus Harbor and grab a few hours' sleep before unloading.

But a hard east wind came up, and on our way in we must have picked up something that fouled our propeller, for when I gave a little throttle to clear the rocky shore, we lost power, and the engine stalled out. Only Tom's quick work with the anchor winch saved us from blowing down on a rocky shore, with no power, a full load of fish, and a dropping tide.

The morning came snappy cold, with stark white frost on the deck and the bell-like ringing of a single halyard against a sailboat's mast in the north wind. We worked two hours, leaning over the stern, sawing away with a knife lashed to an oar. When we began, the propeller was little more than three bronze ears sticking out of a tangled mass of pot warp and the rotted pieces of a lobster trap.

Two hundred "bush" we unloaded in that remote and little-visited spot. Tom and I worked in a steady rhythm, saying little, nor wanting to.

When we threw off the lines and passed outside the breakwater, all Penobscot Bay and the islands opened before us, the water sparkling, the land a tapestry of colors across the horizon. I gave the wheel to Tom and lay down on the foredeck, out of the wind, the October sun full on my face. Now and again I'd look up as we slid through the islands. There were signs of the winter ahead on all sides—lobster traps hauled up on the shore in tidy long piles, summer cottages boarded up, big piles of firewood.

142

It was the last run "east," and we savored it, hustling to unload at each stop, washing down and having a beer as we steamed.

Finally we slid back across the eastern bay, bound for our last stop before home, the lobster co-op at Swan's Island. Tom and I worked fast, for we wanted to be done and headed for home.

"You boys're 'bout done, aren't you?" The manager of the co-op handed us a check and spat over the side of the dock.

I nodded. "Getting hard to get a trip now. This might be it for this year."

"Well, we 'preciate you coming in heres like this. It's hard to get good bait out here. You get another trip, you call me." He stuck out his hand.

"Well," I said, "you helped us out too. I appreciated *that*." The man had saved us more than once when we had more fish than we could sell, taking more bait than he really needed when I called him up.

When we were done and headed west for Vinalhaven, Tom brought up a couple of coffees from the fo'c's'le and we stood there, watching the islands slide past us on both sides.

"It was the last run 'east,' and we savored it."

143

"Pity we didn't do better this year," he said.

I knew the cooler weather was making him think of the winter ahead. It looked like thin times for him and the rest of Jim's herring gang. Despite Jim's immense knowledge and skill at stop seining, they just didn't get the breaks. Their summer had been a bitter one: twice losing schools that would have made their season, then having a big shut-off that no one would buy.

"We were better off last year. There weren't any fish around, but at least what you caught, you could sell. . . . You'd think that maybe if you'd worked since March in this foolish business, you'd at least have enough by November to make it through the winter."

I nodded; if they'd just been able to sell all the fish they shut off in Robert's Harbor, it would have been a season right there.

The last miles: the island ahead, the evening light thin and chill. I turned to Tom. "How's David making out?" I hadn't seen him since the night of the "drug bust."

"Oh, he's holding a turn, I guess. He said he figures you were set up the other night."

"You mean with the Coast Guard?"

"Yeah, the word is that they got an anonymous call." Tom looked over at me. "David figures it was Carl. . . ."

"I hadn't thought of that."

Tom shrugged. "They hit you Friday night. One of David's crew was at the Coast Guard base on Wednesday for something and saw the bulletin board. For Friday it said: 'Board Amaretto.'"

That explained a lot of things.

"What do you think?" I asked him.

"Well, you know, if they *had* found anything," he mused, "at the least they could have tied you up for a while. I mean, compared to buying steaks for an entire seine crew, a phone call is cheap. . . ."

I picked up the binoculars and squinted at a buoy in the distance. The entrance from the east, in through the reefs, was a tricky one. Satisfied, I turned back to Tom, "You know, sometimes that guy gets me so pissed, that if I saw him in the street, I think I'd paste him."

"Go ahead," Tom laughed, "it'd be a real crowd pleaser. . . ."

My competitor was somewhat less than a popular figure along the Vinalhaven waterfront.

The harbor opened up to starboard. It was almost dark. Outside it was too windy to fish, but David's boat was gone. I asked where he might be when everyone else was in.

"Over to the mainland. I guess he's checking on his new boat."

David was having a new, bigger, boat built, so that he would be able to fish for offshore lobster as well as for herring. He hoped to be able to make enough in the good weather months so that he wouldn't have to spend all winter away.

David's mother and I had ridden together once on the ferry, and I had asked her about the new boat, how she felt about it. She looked out the window for a

144

moment before answering, and when she did, it was very different from what I expected.

"My father was a fisherman," she began, "and we lived on Matinicus. When I was a young girl, he built himself a new boat, about the size of this new one of David's. Now there was no radio in those days, or at least he didn't have one. And everyone there on the island was all excited about the new boat.

"But for me, every time he left the harbor to go offshore fishing—for that's what he built the boat for, just like David—I never knew if I'd ever set eyes on him again."

She looked at me for a moment. "And I guess that's about the way I feel about David's new boat. . . ."

I throttled back. The wharf was ahead; the boat slowed.

We slid past David's empty mooring. Lights were going on in houses all around the harbor, and a cold wind was making up; it was a good night to be home. I thought about David again and the uncanny powers he seemed to have as a fisherman. What I had gradually realized out there on those black nights, following him around, was that his skill went beyond mere knowledge of the bottom, the currents, the patterns of fish in years past. When he set out down the bay, what he mostly relied on was a power of perception, of concentration, that he had honed in himself to a level far beyond the rest of us. Eventually I came to believe that he didn't even need the sophisticated electronics that the rest of us would barely leave the dock without, that many nights, he just followed his own finely-tuned instincts to the fish; that he could sense them, feel them.

There are people in many endeavors whose skills border on the super-natural, whose innate abilities go far beyond those produced by experience, training. David was such a man. Yet I wondered if for all his immense talent, it gained him anything in this odd herring game—such as more money, or more time with his family. I wasn't sure that it did.

Another dusk: the clouds thick, the wind strong. When dark came on, David lay alongside us, to wait and listen to the weather, the big boats talking. We hoped that the wind might let go, that it might be a chance after all.

A couple of company carriers were in as well, looking for fish, and as the boats all lay at the wharf, creaking up and down against the pilings in the swell, I spent the evening with Gene, another herring fisherman, in his pickup truck, slowly cruising the island.

Our headlights shone on a world of shuttered-up buildings, wind on grassy fields, boats tossing on their moorings in whitecapped little coves and harbors.

We drank, tossing the empties into the back. The CB radio was on, and every now and then we'd call David back at the boat to see what was going on. But the answer was always the same: "Nope, no chance—least not yet."

So we'd take another turn, go down another road, that led always to the shore and the wind and the black ocean. Finally we stopped on a little hill, near the mouth of the harbor; we could feel the wind, moving and shaking the truck against its springs. Willie Nelson sang "Momma, don't let your sons grow up to

145

be cowboys," and our eyes got accustomed to the black. Far away to the south, beneath the low clouds, we could see the sweep of the beacon from the tall lighthouse on Matinicus Rock and the dim flash of the markers that led us safely back night after night.

"It's not fair, is it?" Gene thumped a thick finger against the windshield.

"What's that?"

"David. All summer long he could get as much as he wanted almost every night down there and hardly sell a boatload. Now he can hardly get down there at all for the weather, and they want everything he can catch."

I shook my head: "No."

At midnight we gave it up, and I went back to the boat. All night long the wind blew the leaves in the streets, and the boats groaned and tugged against their fenders and lines.

Tom and I worked together well—it was better to have a man aboard in the fall. With the wind and the cold, things had a way of happening quickly, and there were times when brute force alone kept us out of a jam. One night at No Man's Land, out in the wind and the sea with no lee at all, we had just come in on David and his net and were trying to lash the corkline to Amaretto's rail when the fish sensed us, all sounded at once. But for Tom and me, pulling together for all we had, we would have lost the corkline—and with it, our load of fish, the only one that David was to find that night.

But the best nights were when we got done early—loaded by ten, tied to the wharf by a little past eleven—and headed up to Tom's house to have a glass of Scotch and a game of darts by the woodstove.

Another rough spell came; on the fourth evening of that southerly blow, I was in Tom's kitchen, the two of us having at the old dart board. Outside, the bare tree limbs clawed at the windows. But after a game and a drink, I drove down to the harbor anyway, just to sit for a moment. I parked at the edge of the wharf, the headlights playing out on the harbor and the dancing boats.

Another truck pulled up beside me in the night. I looked out and saw David; he was out cruising with some of his crew. They rolled down the window, and he saluted me with a paper cup.

"How 'bout going 'fer a sail?"

I looked again at the boats in the pool of our headlights, sailing back and forth in the wind.

"You think it'll be a chance?" I was dubious.

"Down t'the island, might be a lee. . . ."

So I got Tom, and in half an hour the lines were off, and we were on a "chase" with David.

The night was inky. In the pilothouse there was only the dim light on the compass and the glow in the radar tube. On either side of us was the eerie, faint, phosphorescent glow of the seas breaking on the ledges. When we got beyond the reefs and out into the deep water, our bow rose and fell with the seas, and every now and then would dip right into a big one. Brightly glowing little blobs, small comb jellies, they were called, would run down our decks and disappear overboard through the scuppers.

146

Ahead of us, David was only an occasional blotch of phosphorescence as he drove through the seas, throwing spray wide and high.

But he was right as usual. At Seal Island there was a good lee, and we lay there in five or ten acres of smooth, rippled water while the unseen wind sailed by over our heads. There was a good bunch of fish there, too, just as David in his uncanny way knew there would be, and in less than an hour, he had lit up and called me over to load. Once alongside, I dropped my big anchor, for without it the tide would sweep us out of the lee and into the storm that was apparently building outside.

So for an hour, in perhaps the only calm spot of water in hundreds of square miles of ocean, we loaded fish until both holds were filled right up to the top. David came over with the usual paper cups, and looked over the side to see how low in the water we were.

"Better button 'er up good," he said, eyeing our load. "I b'lieve it's still making up out there."

Then he was gone, sailing off into the windy black, and we were left alone in that wild and lonely spot. We tied everything moveable down, even nailed the hatch covers on, and locked the fo'c's'le up tight for the run up the bay before the storm. Once we were underway, Tom steered and I went down into the engine room to check everything over, add oil and water, and just to sit for a bit to see how the old girl did once we got out into the seaway.

Of course everything was fine. The sea was big, but on our stern, and we gently rose and fell as the swells passed beneath us.

But the sight from the top of the engine room ladder will stick in my mind for a long while. There was a single bare bulb at the top of the ladder, and it shone out on a wild and frightening scene. The boat was very low in the water with her load of fish, and seen from the ladder, the water around us was higher than the stern, for it moved in a little valley of its own making. From that angle the seas behind seemed to tower over us, and my first thought was that the next wave was about to come over the stern and into the engine room, and that would be the end of it. Quickly, I climbed up, shut the bottom half of the Dutch door and stood on the top step, watching in horrified fascination.

The seas were traveling faster than the boat, and each time as I watched, the sea behind the boat would get steeper and steeper as it approached, finally looking as if it would totally overpower us. Sometimes water would actually slop over the deck and lap for a moment at the bottom of the Dutch door. But then always Amaretto's stern would rise, and the wave would pass harmlessly beneath us.

Still, there was one time I looked sternward, and for a single moment, behind the pilothouse there was nothing, just the pipe rails sticking out of a smooth hill of black water, rising to an angry-looking top, whipped forward by the wind. For a moment, the stern was under. But for only a moment, and then it was lifting clear, water pouring out of the freeing ports in the low bulwarks. I picked my moment between seas, went out and closed both top and bottom of the Dutch door tightly, then crept around into the pilothouse.

"Wild one, isn't it?" Tom said, a noticeable tightness in his voice.

"You bet. How'd she handle?"

"Oh, all right," he exhaled heavily, "but I don't think I'd want any more."

The radio spoke. It was David.

"How you boys makin' it?" Clearly over the radio we heard the rush of the wind in through the sides of his open pilothouse and the rise and fall of the engine as his boat alternately slid down and nosed up the shoulder of a great sea.

"Ah, it's quite . . . wild right here . . . David, but we're making it OK. . . . I don't know that I'd want any more though."

"Nooooo . . . I don't b'lieve I would either. . . . It's not a fit night for anything but being home. . . ."

"Then what are we doing out in it?"

"Ahhh . . ." he said, his voice totally relaxed despite the wild night outside and his much smaller boat, "the greed of the herring fisherman, it boggles the mind. . . ."

A little while passed. I slid out and around into the engine room again to check the bilge, but it was dry; if we were making any water, the little automatic pump was taking care of it.

The wind ripped a narrow opening in the clouds above us; a moment later, it closed it. But the swollen moon burst through, shone upon the wild scene around us, and I thought I could see David, a little way ahead; he looked as if he had slowed down, waiting for us, making sure we were still behind.

The way home was a narrow, dark strip of deep water between heavily breaking ledges and reefs, dimly seen in night and rain. But it was a road we had taken many times before, and when we finally made our turn, the sea died away beneath us, the harbor opened up, and we breathed a little easier. I made out David, rowing alone across the harbor, his boat already on the mooring, his crew dropped off on the dock. Then we slid alongside the wharf, shut down, and were done.

Just at the top of the wharf, I stopped for a moment before getting into Tom's truck. The wind and the rain were living things then, clutching at my oilskins, rattling the old fish plant beside me, and there was something else clearly heard, the loud booming of the sea on the outer ledges. The storm was a big one, much worse than when we had left, unexpected, unforecast. Then the truck started up, the headlights stabbing out onto a wild scene of a whitecapped harbor, with fifty or sixty boats all straining at their moorings, and it was time to go.

When I think of David, it is just this night that I think about. Black, windy, all the other boats in. And David, out cruising in his truck, looking out at the night, feeling the fish down at the island, knowing they were there. Finally getting his crew together, tracking us down, and sailing out into the black. Steaming ten miles with every sea right over the bow, then still in stygian black, sliding into a lee where he knew there'd be one, and finding that bunch of fish that he knew had to be there.

148

Fourteen

Some years there are fish through November, into December even; the weather stays warm. But that fall was cool, and the water lost its heat fast. From the outer coves all the dories were in, and in the harbor itself only a few were left, against the odd chance of a school of stragglers wandering into a cove. And around the shore, at breakfast and in the fish houses, the talk was of "west'ard"—of Gloucester, Portsmouth, Cape Cod, where the fish would be in the winter.

There was a peculiar sound to the wind after the leaves were gone. In the summer and early fall, the leaves had kept the wind off the ground, above the houses even. But by late October the wind was lower, clawing around the houses and in the streets, and when it blew, it did so with a new sound, a sort of roar.

But that last night two company carriers were in anyway. That was the end of it for them, that week the last for sure. I didn't think they'd do much business, for the wind was nor'west, cold and gusty. They lay beside Amaretto while I worked in the engine room, cleaning up, putting things away, for I didn't know if we'd get another trip or not. But then I heard them start up. I went up to see them throwing the lines off and David's boat disappearing into the windy dark at the mouth of the harbor.

Henry waved to me out the pilothouse door. "Well, we'll go and have a look at it anyway. C'mon along, Joe; you might get a trip."

I shook my head. What with the wind and them ahead of me for the fish, my chances of getting a trip were slim. Besides, if there were fish close, and a lee to fish them in, I could be there in an hour.

"Naw, I'm just gonna keep the radio on and see what happens. . . ."

He nodded and then they were off, gone into the night. But just an hour later, I could hear the radio talking and went up to listen. It was David. Already he had a set, down in a lee by Green Islands; he was calling the other carriers in. It sounded like he had a lot of fish, so I called him.

"David, what's it look like?"

"Ahhhh . . . plenty of fish here. . . . Give it to 'er, Joe; it's a good chance. . . ."

So I got Tom and we set out, around the corner and down the bay on a windy black night when I'd about given up on getting another trip.

We saw their lights when we were halfway down, and finally came around the corner of the island to find the second carrier already low in the water, almost full, anchored alongside David in the tiniest of lees, just room for the net and the two of them and little else. On one side was the rocky shore of the island; and on the other, the wind, kicking up a wicked short chop.

Then the carrier was done. It hauled up its anchor and backed away, not getting fifty yards before it began to wallow heavily in the sea and swell.

David waved us in, and we slid alongside, anchored, made his corkline fast to our rail, and began brailing. He came aboard, passing me a paper cup when I took a break from the rhythm of loading.

"Hell of a set, David. . . ." I nodded down to the fish still in the net. He had already loaded two boats twice my size and still had enough to load me.

He shrugged. "It's about the end of it. These fish're traveling. . . ."

I looked around when I got a chance. This set reminded me of the last one we had gotten from him, except that at Seal Island, the lee had been a big one, encompassing the entire north side of the island. Here, the island was nothing more than a dot, with a lee about the size of a house lot. Into this tiny pinhole David had slipped, finding the only place in tonight's wind and tide where a net could be safely set. We were at least six miles from the nearest land on any side. No one had been here in at least a week; even the plane had not seen such a bunch of fish all together in one spot for weeks. The man's power was uncanny.

Henry Dodge, skipper of the carrier Pauline: "C'mon along, Joe; you might get a trip."

151

We sipped our drinks, and David looked away to the west at the dimly-seen masthead lights of the two other carriers, making wide arcs in the black as they rolled their way across the bay to the mainland.

"Two trips they took," he said. "Good fish too,"—he spat over the rail—"but we'll be lucky to be paid for one. . . ."

It was the first time he had mentioned the new arrangement with the sardine canneries—paying the fishermen only for what the canneries said they "used" rather than for what they took. The fishermen didn't have much choice—most of them owed money to the canneries, and besides, there was no one else to buy their fish, except for little shoestring operations like ours which never really amounted to much.

He didn't say any more. When we were done, he went back aboard his boat, and in minutes, they were just a light, rising and falling in the black as they bucked their way up the bay for home.

When Amaretto was all cleaned up finally and headed for home, the wind made the steel stays sing and rattled spray against the windows.

Somewhere between Monhegan Island and Mt. Desert Rock, between June and October, we had made a season. It had come in bits and pieces, and for the longest time, I hadn't expected it to come at all. I thought that we would have to go to Gloucester or Portsmouth to lug herring all winter. It wouldn't be an easy berth for an old boat.

It wasn't a big season we'd made, but I could pay the bills and get through the winter. For now, that was enough.

The stars were bright, and the wind had a new edge to it that night. There might have been a few more fish to be had, but to me, it seemed as good a time to quit as any.

A little before noon on a blustery fall day, I shoveled the last herring into the basket, called for Tom to hoist away, stood up to ease the pain in my back, and our season was done.

I spent the afternoon with the hose and the brush, scrubbing every bit of the topsides, washing out the holds again and again to get the very last of the blood and herring smell out, cleaning every last herring scale off the sides of the pilothouse.

The breeze dropped out, and the day grew wonderfully warm. Above me as I worked I could see three of the older fishermen of the island sitting on the pier, looking down on Amaretto and smiling, enjoying the Indian summer afternoon. As I moved forward, starting to scrub the sides of the fo'c's'le hatch, I could hear the men on the dock calling out to one another, saying how good the boat looked just then and reminiscing about the times she had come to the island when they were young, who was the skipper on her then, how much herring they had and where they got them, who they worked with.

And if there are pieces of those seasons with Amaretto that I want to hold onto and remember, that would surely be one of them. In the clear, still air, I could hear the ringing of hammers over at the boatyard, as men readied their boat cradles for the winter storage season. The lobsterboats that had gone out to haul that morning would still be another hour before returning, and for the moment, the harbor was still, a pattern of skiffs and mooring buoys. The wind and the rain had washed the air clean, and the houses around the harbor stood out sharp and clear, the scene starkly different, beautiful in a new way with the leaves about gone.

Cornwallis trailed me around the boat as I worked, but the heat got to him, making him loggy, slow. Finally he plopped down and passed out in a big pool of sunlight.

There are other pieces I want to hold: a night at Seal Island, with a great bonfire dying out and the voices of men and their families as they camped, watching the great school of fish they had trapped in the cove below them. The voices growing more and more hushed as the night came on black and the fish started to move in the water below, making it glow and fire with their passage, an unforgettable sight. Then, later that night, on Amaretto, going out on deck, shivering in the chill, trying to remember the sound that had brought me on deck. Then hearing it again—humpback whales, breathing close at hand, then suddenly visible—big as locomotives, shimmering with phosphorescence, sliding slowly back and forth along the edge of the net.

Another night, Monhegan Island, lying at the wharf, radar and radios on, engine slowly ticking over. And men and women, in fancy dress, just down from dinner at the hotel, standing on the wharf and peering curiously at us, wondering what it was about the night, the boat, that gave the moment such a mysterious air. Then the radio spoke and the lines were off, and in a moment we were in a world as different as night is from day, surrounded by nothing but gray, swirling fog. Then finally, a circle of light, a boat, and men looking down into the water, waiting.

Another island, lost in time, with fog and sheep and tumbledown buildings, waist-high in grass.

A cove with more fish than anyone had seen in years, uneasy men in dories, closing it all off with a wall of net, working frantically to secure it with lines and anchors. Then the pale hunter's moon rising above the ridge, and the first light touching the water, driving the fish mad till they tore through the nets, the water in a frenzy.

And David again, just three nights ago, calling me on the radio: "Give it to 'er, Joe; it's a good chance. . . ." Finding him in a tiny lee, when it had been a week since anyone had seen a fish, loading three boats with a single set of the net. But knowing in his own mind, more surely than any biologist, that it was the end, the last of the season around the bay.

When I first began this business, I thought it might have grace—my 1918 boat with its 1942 engine, working again, doing what it had been built for. I pictured a hard but honest living. But then when I got into it a bit, I saw it as something else—a cutthroat racket, aesthetically and morally bankrupt: loading as many fish as you could, peddling them for all you could get, dumping the rest.

But after a while, I saw that I had been right the first time. The business was far from perfect, but there *was* a certain grace to it. Most of it had to do with the boat, for this was what she had been built to do, this the coast that for sixty years she had plied, the harbor that for sixty years had seen her come and go.

And just that afternoon, seeing Amaretto lying at the island wharf, the men above her talking, I understood what I had sensed in Friendship Harbor that July evening when our journey had at last begun. Put into words, it would be something like this—that boats may have destinies, just as people do. That all those wonderfully skilled workers who had put her together in East Boothbay in 1918, and all her skippers down through the years, and the towns and people up and down the coast that had depended on her, had put into her, if not some sort of life, then at least some sort of power.

It was a power that reached out, caused me to buy a boat I had seen only once before. And then to spend all my money, borrow even more. It was a power that brought strangers down to the boat again and again, lending us stuff, giving us stuff, in that improbable chain of events that had brought us here.

And once we got to Vinalhaven, anything could have stopped us. We were on the thinnest of shoestrings; another boat had the market sewed up tight. I had put the entire boat together—wiring, plumbing, hydraulics—with only the shakiest concept of how it should be done. And it had all worked flawlessly.

I woke the dog. We walked around to the far side of the harbor. From there Amaretto, lying at the wharf, was backed by row after row of neat white houses, with delicate tracings of gingerbread woodwork and carved shingles.

Truly she looked as if she had come home.

And finally, on a nippy first of November morning, it was time to go.

I picked up my mail, walked with Cornwallis back to the boat, past stores with soaped-up windows from Halloween the night before. I thanked Tom for all that he had done, wished him a good winter.

Then with little fanfare, I threw the lines off, and we slid out past the boats and the lobster buying stations, around the point, and into the shining bay.

The sun rose in the sky and the ocean was still. The mainland, the islands, the reefs, and the lobster buoys stood out starkly against blue sky and water. Those islands which in night and fog had seemed so mysterious were revealed as placid places of rock and sand and grass, rising from a glassy blue plain.

When we made South Bristol, Junior was there, patching some twine on his wharf. He took my lines, asked how we'd done.

And when I told him, he said, "Good. She made out, then. We all hoped she would. . . ."

I shut down the engine and hoisted Cornwallis up the ladder, for his dogger friends were waiting. There was the familiar rattle of a car going over the little swing bridge, the sound of grinders over at the shipyard, and I looked around and thought of Seal Island and No Man's Land, Matinicus Rock and Hurricane Sound, all those places where we had spent so much time. Though they were but six or seven hours away by boat, and though we had just left them that morning, how very, very far away they seemed.

Fifteen

In early November David's newest Starlight was ready, a graceful, glass fifty-five-footer. It was a slack time in the herring fishery just then, so he took two men with him and moved load after load of lobster traps offshore to fish the mouths of the "canyons," those great fissures in the continental shelf leading down to the deeps. They'd steam off, run for twenty hours into open ocean, their only points of reference the flickering numbers on a Loran set. Far from land, they would run through their "string," hauling the pots, moving the ones that weren't fishing well. When they were done, it would be a fifteen-hour steam to the west to sell at Portsmouth, New Hampshire, and finally an eight- or ten-hour steam up the coast for home. More often than not, they'd roll the net back aboard when they got home and go out searching for herring.

I had the feeling it was a hard time in David's life just then, trying to do two fisheries at once, but I guessed he was used to burning the candle at both ends. He'd been at it about a month when I ran into him one day, and was struck by how much he seemed to have aged. I asked him how he liked the offshore business.

"It's a city out there now," he said, in his husky voice, his sky-blue eyes looking ancient and tired. "I used to like it. Last winter wasn't too bad, even in the old Starlight. But now, you lie out there a hundred miles from shore, trying to sleep a few hours in the middle of the night, and it's like a city with all the other boats out there, doing the same thing. Just like a city."

For a while after that I mostly lost track of the herring business. From time to time I'd get the fish news through the grapevine, and now and again I'd see Tom, or one of the others, headed back from Gloucester for a weekend.

Then, in December, the herring market picked up. David brought his lobster gear back in and started fishing pretty hard out of Gloucester. They had a few good weeks there, and then the fish moved north to a lonely spot called the Isles of Shoals. David, Jim, and their men moved with them, fishing for a while out of Portsmouth, New Hampshire.

One week in mid-December I had to make a trip down to Boston, and stopped in on them in Portsmouth on the way back up to Maine. We met in a bar on the shore of the Piscataqua River. The herring boys were all at a couple of tables by the big windows overlooking the river. Outside, the early winter dusk was lost in the coming night, and I could see the current swirl in the black water.

"It's got the strongest current of any river in the east," Tom said. "It really boils, sucks the buoys right under." He and the others were staying in motels around town. Their seiners and the carriers lay at a wharf right in front of the bar and restaurant. It was a pretty cozy arrangement: the men could come down in the evening, eat, catch the weather report, look out at the wind on the river, and see if the night would bring a chance or not.

It had become a mean and cold winter, and I was glad I wasn't down there, hanging around, far from home, for a few nights' fishing a week. I admired them for it, but I knew that if they had had any kind of a season around the island, they'd be back there now. It was just good fortune that Amaretto and I weren't down there with them, too.

One of the men looked out the window at the black river. "If it looks good, we can get rigged up in insulated coveralls and be out the door and down the river in a few minutes."

Three miles downriver was the ocean, and five miles off to the south were the Isles of Shoals, where more often than not, there would be a sizable bunch of fish. On a good night, they could slip out, be fishing an hour and a half after they left the dock, get a trip, and be back in before a storm blew up.

"But it can come up real quick, too," Tom said, pointing out to the Nighthawk: the rigging was encrusted in thick, white ice. "The Delca was pumping, already half-loaded when the wind started to blow. They really needed the fish, so we stayed until they got their trip. But soon as we were done and clear of the lee of the islands, we knew it was going to be a hard chance to get back. Close to the land, it came off cold, and we made ice, heavy. The rigging, the radar, everything iced up wicked thick. It came on so fast, we made all that ice so quick, it was a worry. . . ." His voice trailed off and I looked out at the ghostly, iced-up rigging again.

"But there was nowhere to go, so we kept going, Jim sticking his head outside every now and then to see where we were. . . . We thought that once we made it up into the river, we'd be OK, but the wind was nor'west and just smoking down the river from the mountains inland. The sea was down, but man, that spray was just like a hose gushing over everything, freezing on everything it touched. . . ."

One of the other men spoke. "You'd look ashore and see people in their windows watching TV, and woodsmoke out of their chimneys, and there we were, right up against it, still makin' ice. . . . I tell you, if it'd been any worse, I'd been 'fer puttin' 'er ashore. . . . That's how rotten it was. . . ."

"And an hour later we were sitting in here, puttin' the hot rums to us and looking out at that mess." Tom yanked his head out the window at the iced-up boat.

I asked how David had made out in Gloucester with his new boat, and there were smiles all around the table.

"Those Gloucester guys couldn't believe the likes of David. They were all used to their big boats and deep nets, and along comes David with a little shallow net, setting places they didn't think *anyone* could, and most nights loading his carrier and heading in before they even had a fish!"

"And one night he was out sailing around reading a magazine, not really even paying attention, and stumbled across a big bunch and loaded three carriers when no one else had anything for the whole night. . . ."

The rest of the men smiled. They enjoyed telling stories about David. I could tell they were proud of him.

There were a few hardbitten-looking guys sitting over in one corner of the bar, away from the rest of the Maine boys. I asked one of the guys about them. They were David's crew, I was told.

157

"David's gang?" I was amazed. They were a far cry from the husky gang he fished with at home. "What happened to the others?"

"Quit."

"How come?" It didn't make sense.

"Well. . . ." The speaker paused; it seemed as if he didn't really know exactly how to explain it. "I guess there's been a lot of pressure on him. . . ."

"What kind of pressure?"

"Well, you know, money pressure and all—that new boat's got some pretty hefty payments that go along with it. And with the sardine companies giving everybody such a screwing these last couple of years, he's had to really drive. . . ."

"And . . .?"

"And, well, some guys feel he's been taking chances . . . more than he ever did before."

"So his gang quit, after fishing with him for years," I said. "I thought they'd be dying to get on a new boat like that." It didn't really make sense to me. When I knew them, they all had been tremendously loyal to David. Things would have to be pretty terrible before they'd quit.

"Well . . . they'd had some close calls, and then last week, they had a real big set of fish and were out there loading the Delca, with a strain on the boom from the weight of the fish and all. The topping lift on the boom broke, and the whole works came crashing down on the deck of the carrier. The guys I talked to said the boat would have rolled over for sure if that carrier hadn't been there. . . . It scared 'em . . . so now he's got this bunch. . . ."

The men in the corner stood up. I looked around and saw that David had come into the bar. He was dressed in black. He spotted me and came over; we spoke a few words, and then he was gone out the door with his crew. He looked tired and gaunt, even more so than the last time I had seen him. But there was about him that curious quality I had always noted before when he was out looking for fish—a totally relaxed, almost distant feeling.

And more—I felt this keenly, even if but for a moment. It was as if the bitter, windy night, the unfamiliar crew, the new boat with bugs yet to be worked out hardly existed. I sensed clearly, standing there, talking to him for a few minutes, what I had first heard about him the winter before. It was as if he knew the fish were out there, and exactly where. In an odd way, just for a moment, I felt keenly that he was waiting for them, and they for him.

Then the feeling was gone. I looked out the window. The Starlight's engine started up with a little puff of white smoke, and David's men were working on the stern, getting the net ready, untying the lines from the dock.

Out beyond the boats and the dock, there was a lot of wind on the water. It didn't seem like much of a night. But standing off in the chop raised by the wind pushing against the current was a big factory carrier, faintly outlined by her running lights.

I thought again about all the fish that David could have caught for them a few months before, when they were around Seal Island and the weather was good. I watched the latest Starlight move away from the dock, gathering way, the current pushing her downstream, watched until her lights were lost around the bend.

A little snow squall swept down the river, blotting out the cold world outside for a moment. I turned to Tom. "You guys going out?"

"Oh, maybe," he said. "Jim'll be down by and by. But David's our weatherman these nights. . . . If he doesn't think it's too bad, we'll probably slide out and have a look at it."

I talked to a few of the other men, wished them luck, and left. Home was still three hours down the road. Outside it was dark, windy, and very cold.

A few weeks passed before I saw any of them again. Sometimes Tom would call up late at night from the bar, when they weren't going out. He was homesick for the island, I could tell, and the weather was getting worse. He said they'd take off a few days at Christmastime, and then hit 'er again, hoping to get all they could before January and the real hard weather came on. Someone told me that David was really driving hard, going out in some awful weather. Even his new gang got shook up a few times, when they had been caught on the outside after all the others had run for shelter.

There was a thaw around Christmas, and then two days later it came off cold for a week—bitter cold and windy. The harbors froze over, and I was glad for an insulated house and a good woodpile. Then, the first week in January, Tom called from Vinalhaven to say they were done, and I took a day and went out to see him.

David was on the ferry, his truck parked right up on the bow, behind the steel chains. He honked when he saw me, and waved me in. The truck heater had the cab toasty, and he poured me a full cup of coffee brandy, for it was bitter cold and mean outside.

I noticed for the first time that he wore hearing aids in both ears, and I asked him about it.

He shrugged. "Noisy engines. . . ."

But he looked good, real good, and I was both surprised and pleased for him. He said little, but whatever it was that had aged him, wearing him down and causing him to go through his crews, seemed to have passed. The ferry slid through the sea smoke that shrouded the frigid bay, and David told me he had only come to get a few things from home. He was heading back to Portsmouth for the rest of the winter, even if the weather would allow him just a trip a week. He needed the money.

I asked him about his family, about the talk I had heard of problems at home. I knew that the new boat, the constant fishing, and being away so much had put a real strain on things. We were passing through the White Islands and into Hurricane Sound just then, the prettiest part of the whole trip, a place where we had snuck around in the black and the fog, night after night, chasing David or someone else after a few herring.

"No," he said, "that's all better now. I've even got my old crew back again. But for a while it looked as if I'd end up living in my dad's shop." He made a wry smile.

The ferry passed through the narrows east of Hurricane Sound, rounded the

159

point, and slowed for the harbor. From where we sat on the bow of the ferry, I could see to the very head of the harbor, to David's father's home and the shop of which David spoke. It stood on a little rise behind the house, a simple building, sixteen by twenty feet at the most, with a woodstove, a workbench, a bunch of half-made lobster pots, a pile of herring twine, and who knows what else. But the window gave out on the cove below and the harbor beyond, and because it was a little higher than the land around, it commanded a view of the bay, too. And though I hadn't been inside, I supposed even Seal Island, No Man's Land, and the other distant islands around which David had spent so much of his life could be seen.

I turned to him. "You could do worse, David."

He smiled a slow smile, as if what I had said had just occurred to him.

"Yeah," he said, "I guess you're right."

Then the ferry slid into the landing, the ramp was down, and in the early winter dusk I could see Tom waiting, stamping his feet in the cold, and it was time to go.

*   *   *   *   *

Seal Island, the next year: storm petrels swooped and dived, surrounding Amaretto as she lay at anchor. She was freshly painted, and banners streamed from her mast. We had come to look and wait for fish, but for something else too. A lobsterman, one of the first to buy bait from us, was aboard, as were his wife and some other friends.

Just at seven o'clock Ann stepped up out of the fo'c's'le in her wedding dress with a necklace of flowers. She took her place on the foredeck, beside her mother, and then Tom stepped out of the pilothouse in a dark suit, a single white carnation on his lapel.

They stood together beneath the mast, and the justice of the peace, a man who had also worked aboard Amaretto, spoke the graceful words that bound them together.

Above us, around us, the gulls cried out to one another, and the storm petrels made their soft callings. There was rum and wine and champagne at the edge of night, and afterward a salmon in the cozy fo'c's'le.

When it was full night, the fog came in around us. While the others slept, I got into my old clothes and started up the engine as quietly as I could. Tom met me on the foredeck, and we hauled the anchor together and set out through the night and fog once more, to chase after the "wily kipper," to get a load of fish.

*   *   *   *   *

And Amaretto again, one last time; this shouldn't happen ever, to any boat. It is 1985, deep in a July night. An outboard skiff appears out of the black, reverses softly beside her at the wharf. There is something odd about this—a man very quietly steps aboard, as if he doesn't want to be heard or seen. He checks the

160

fo'c's'le and pilothouse to see if anyone is aboard, and when he is sure the boat is deserted, moves quickly, starting the engine, taking in the lines.

She idles out of the harbor, out into the western bay. There is a fish pump on her stern now, and the man starts it up, but there is no seiner or net in sight. He lowers the heavy hose into the water and arranges the discharge so that the water is pouring into the fish holds.

Lower she sinks in the water, and lower. When the holds are full, the man directs the water into the fo'c's'le, and as that fills the whole forward part of the boat is awash. He quickly steps into the engine room to make sure that it is filling too, as the water from the fo'c's'le runs aft through the bilges.

Satisfied, he brings the skiff alongside, steps aboard, and motors quickly toward the mainland shore a few miles away, stopping once a short distance off to look back. With a kind of a snuffle, Amaretto's engine stops as the water covers the blower intake, and in less than a minute she is gone.

Our little boy, Matthew, took the news hard. He was just two and a half then, talking a lot, most of it about boats. My wife, Mary Lou, and I had built a house on the shore of Old Harbor, looking out at Hurricane Sound and the White Islands. In the afternoons when the lobsterboats came in from hauling they'd pass right below the house, and Matthew would be out there waving.

Amaretto was still Matthew's favorite boat. I had sold her a few years before, and Tom and I were now partners in a little dragger. But it was still good to see her sliding in across Hurricane Sound, plugged with herring from a night down the bay, or tied up at the wharf in Carver's Harbor with a dozen lobsterboats waiting, as they had waited for us.

Whenever Matthew saw her, he'd call out to anybody who'd listen, "Dere daddy's 'ole boat. . . ."

Baiting was still as cutthroat as ever. Whoever stole and sank her probably figured that with her gone, he'd have more market for himself. I tried to explain to Matthew what had happened to her, but I wasn't sure he understood.

Then someone was over for a visit who hadn't heard the news but remembered Matthew's interest in the boat.

"Where's Amaretto, Matthew?"

"Sank."

"Who did it?"

"Bad man."

161

Epilogue

Traditionally, when the young herring moved into the inshore waters of the Gulf of Maine each summer, fishermen using a variety of gear and methods all had a crack at them. The weir fishermen of Eastern Maine, the stop-seine fishermen the length of the coast, and the purse seiners would all usually manage to piece together their seasons from the fish available. For the most part, the herring fishermen made their livings in sight of their home ports; it was a way of fishing and a way of life that had gone on for most of the century.

In the 1960s, however, the appearance of a fleet of large, primarily Eastern European vessels catching herring in the offshore waters of Georges Bank changed the complexion of the herring fishery—probably forever. Although it was inadequately understood at the time, the offshore herring that these vessels were catching in such large numbers were the parents of the juvenile fish upon which the Maine inshore fishery is based.

There followed years of very low catches, and the weir and stop-seine fishermen found themselves at a disadvantage. Being limited by geography and the nature of their gear, these men had to wait for the fish to come to them. The purse seine fishermen responded by building bigger boats and longer and deeper nets. The larger vessels enabled them to range farther afield, but with the burden of larger mortgage payments. The payments had to be met, and it became very difficult for the owners to stay in their home ports after the herring moved south in the fall.

The larger vessels and nets only made things worse for the stop-seine fishermen. Vessels from as far away as Gloucester could quickly scoop up a body of fish that, left to their own devices, might have moved inshore to coves where the stop seiners could have caught them.

One effect of all these changes was to force the herring fishermen farther and farther from home. The Vinalhaven fishermen who spent their winters fishing out of Portsmouth and Gloucester would have preferred to be home with their families, but the fish and the market just weren't there in the summer anymore.

The relationship between the fishermen and the sardine canneries had always been a close one. The canneries often advanced the fishermen money in the spring to get their gear ready, and a casual "open-door" relationship between plant management and fishermen allowed disputes to be resolved quickly.

In the mid-Seventies a Texas conglomerate, for whatever unfathomable reasons, bought up two of the larger sardine companies, and with that single transaction, for many fishermen, the old ways vanished. "It used to be you could just walk right into the office if you had a problem," one fisherman told me. "And then it changed, and they had to consult Houston before you could even buy a piece o' twine."

163

The relationship between fishermen and canneries deteriorated even further when many fishermen joined in a lawsuit against the sardine companies for illegal pricing and buying practices.

Meanwhile, changes were taking place in the food business, changes to which the sardine companies, being conservative, were slow to react. Canned sardines, the "working man's lunch" of the 1950s, were less in tune with the consumer of the '70's. During the years of very low catches, many of the women in the cannery workforce found better, more year-round employment. Cutting herring for sardines is a skilled task, and when, finally, a few more fish began to appear along the coast, the canneries were often unable to hire enough packers. The smaller sardine companies in particular suffered from inflation and high interest rates. Rising costs of operation and of financing warehouses full of canned product ate up whatever small margins there had been.

In 1976, when I bought Amaretto, there were six operating sardine canneries buying from Penobscot Bay fishermen. In 1984, the Holmes Packing Company plant in Rockland burned, lighting up the sky for miles around in a spectacular blaze. It was not rebuilt. A few months later, a quarter of a mile away, the North Lubec Packing Company closed its doors for the last time.

The year before, the Royal River Packing Company in Yarmouth was shut down and sold to nonfishing interests. In the spring of 1986, as I finish this book, just three plants are left in the midcoast area.